# STEPHEN KING

**Recent Titles in**
**Critical Companions to Popular Contemporary Writers**
Kathleen Gregory Klein, Series Editor

Mary Higgins Clark: A Critical Companion
*Linda C. Pelzer*

Michael Crichton: A Critical Companion
*Elizabeth A. Trembley*

V. C. Andrews: A Critical Companion
*E. D. Huntley*

Anne McCaffrey: A Critical Companion
*Robin Roberts*

Pat Conroy: A Critical Companion
*Landon C. Burns*

John Saul: A Critical Companion
*Paul Bail*

James Clavell: A Critical Companion
*Gina Macdonald*

# STEPHEN KING

## *A Critical Companion*

Sharon A. Russell

CRITICAL COMPANIONS TO POPULAR CONTEMPORARY WRITERS
Kathleen Gregory Klein, Series Editor

**Greenwood Press**
**Westport, Connecticut • London**

**Library of Congress Cataloging-in-Publication Data**

Russell, Sharon A.
Stephen King : a critical companion / Sharon A. Russell.
p. cm.—(Critical companions to popular contemporary writers, ISSN 1082–4979)
Includes bibliographical references (p. ) and index.
ISBN 0–313–29417–8 (alk. paper)
1. King, Stephen, 1947- —Criticism and interpretation.
2. Horror tales, American—History and criticism. I. Title.
II. Series.
PS3561.I483Z865 1996
813'.54—dc20 95–50460



British Library Cataloguing in Publication Data is available.



Library of Congress Catalog Card Number: 95–50460
ISBN: 0–313–29417–8
ISSN: 1082–4979

First published in 1996

Greenwood Press, 88 Post Road West, Westport, CT 06881
An imprint of Greenwood Publishing Group, Inc.

Printed in the United States of America

The paper used in this book complies with the Permanent Paper Standard issued by the National Information Standards Organization (Z39.48–1984).

10 9 8 7 6 5 4 3 2 1

For my sister Judith, who shares my love of the horror genre. She has fought many monsters in her life.

## *ADVISORY BOARD*

# Contents

# Series Foreword

The authors who appear in the series Critical Companions to Popular Contemporary Writers are all best-selling writers. They do not have only one successful novel, but a string of them. Fans, critics, and specialist readers eagerly anticipate their next book. For some, high cash advances and breakthrough sales figures are automatic; movie deals often follow. Some writers become household names, recognized by almost everyone.

But novels are read one by one. Each reader chooses to start and, more importantly, to finish a book because of what she or he finds there. The real test of a novel is in the satisfaction its readers experience. This series acknowledges the extraordinary involvement of readers and writers in creating a best-seller.

The authors included in this series were chosen by an Advisory Board composed of high school English teachers and high school and public librarians. They ranked a list of best-selling writers according to their popularity among different groups of readers. Writers in the top-ranked group who had not received book-length, academic literary analysis (or none in at least the past ten years) were chosen for the series. Because of this selection method, Critical Companions to Popular Contemporary Writers meets a need that is not addressed elsewhere.

The volumes in the series are written by scholars with particular expertise in analyzing popular fiction. These specialists add an academic focus to the popular success that the best-selling writers already enjoy.

The series is designed to appeal to a wide range of readers. The general reading public will find explanations for the appeal of these well-known writers. Fans will find biographical and fictional questions answered. Students will find literary analysis, discussions of fictional genres, carefully organized introductions to new ways of reading the novels, and bibliographies for additional research. Students will also be able to apply what they have learned from this book to their readings of future novels by these best-selling writers.

Each volume begins with a biographical chapter drawing on published information, and biographies or memoirs, prior interviews, and, in some cases, interviews given especially for this series. A chapter on literary history and genres describes how the author's work fits into a larger literary content. The following chapters analyze the writer's most important, most popular, and most recent novels in detail. Each chapter focuses on a single novel. This approach, suggested by the Advisory Board as the most useful to student research, allows for an in-depth analysis of the writer's fiction. Close and careful readings with numerous examples show readers exactly how the novels work. These chapters are organized around three central elements: plot development (how the story line moves forward), character development (what the reader knows about the important figures), and theme (the significant ideas of the novel). Chapters may also include sections on generic conventions (how the novel is similar to or different from others in its same category of science fiction, fantasy, thriller, etc.), narrative point of view (who tells the story and how), symbols and literary language, and historical or social context. Each chapter ends with an "alternative reading" of the novel. The volume concludes with a primary and secondary bibliography, including reviews.

The Alternative Readings are a unique feature of this series. By demonstrating a particular way of reading each novel, they provide a clear example of how a specific perspective can reveal important aspects of the book. In each alternative reading section, one contemporary literary theory—such as feminist criticism, Marxism, new historicism, deconstruction, or Jungian psychological critique—is defined in brief, easily comprehensible language. That definition is then applied to the novel to highlight specific features that might go unnoticed or be understood differently in a more general reading of the novel. Each volume defines two or three specific theories, making them part of the reader's understanding of how diverse meanings may be constructed from a single novel.

Taken collectively, the volumes in the Critical Companions to Popular Contemporary Writers series provide a wide-ranging investigation of the complexities of current best-selling fiction. By treating these novels seriously as both literary works and publishing successes, the series demonstrates the potential of popular literature in contemporary culture.

Kathleen Gregory Klein
Southern Connecticut State University

# Acknowledgments

I would like to thank all of my students who have shared their love of Stephen King with me. I would also like to thank Carolyn Morris, a great King fan and office manager, who has helped make it possible for me to write this book.

# STEPHEN KING

1

# The Life of Stephen King

Stephen King's life and work are examples of both traditional and modern views of the American Dream. The story of his early life resembles tales about children born in poverty who grow up to be president or head of a big company. Moving from city to city and being raised by a single parent are also hardships familiar to many contemporary Americans. In order to understand King's achievements and his outlook on his work, we have to examine both sides of the American Dream as it works itself out in his life. King is one of America's most popular contemporary authors. He is also one of the few who is easily recognized by the general public. Even before cinematic adaptations of his work appeared, fans knew him. At the same time he manages to live a relatively normal life in Maine. While he tries to guard his privacy so that he has time to write, he has been very generous with interviews. He has also reflected on his life and work in articles, in introductions to his books, and in his nonfiction study of the horror genre, *Danse Macabre*. How he deals with fame and his work in the horror genre is the subject of an essay called "On Becoming a Brand Name" in an early collection of essays about him, *Fear Itself*.

## EARLY LIFE

King is a member of the baby boom generation. After Donald Edwin King returned from World War II, he and his wife, Nellie Ruth Pillsbury

King, adopted a son, David Victor, on September 14, 1945. Doctors had told them they could not have children of their own. But as many adoptive parents have discovered, the doctors were wrong. Stephen was born two years later, on September 21, 1947, at the Maine General Hospital in Portland (Beahm, *Stephen King Story* 15). King's mother was of Scottish descent and claimed to be related to the famous Pillsburys who make flour and related items. "The difference between the two branches, Mom said, was that the flour-Pillsburys moved west to make their fortune, while our people stayed shirttail but honest on the coast of Maine" (*Danse* 98). While not famous, his grandmother was the first woman to graduate from Gorham Normal School, and his grandfather worked for a short time for Winslow Homer, the artist (*Danse* 98). King's father's family came from Ireland and settled in Peru, Indiana.

When Stephen was two years old his father went out for a pack of cigarettes and never returned. While King never knew his father, he saw photographs of him and is certain he inherited his poor eyesight (*Danse* 99). After his father left, his mother supported the family with a variety of jobs. They had few material possessions but never went hungry. "She was a talented pianist and a woman with a great and sometimes eccentric sense of humor and somehow she kept things together, as women before her have done and as other women are doing even now as we speak" (*Danse* 99). The family moved around the country for the next nine years, always remaining poor. They stayed with relatives, most often those on his mother's side, in such cities as Malden, Massachusetts; Stratford, Connecticut; Chicago, Illinois; West De Pere, Wisconsin; and Fort Wayne, Indiana (Beahm, *Stephen King Companion* 16). The family finally returned to Durham, Maine, when his grandparents were in their eighties, and his mother was hired to take care of them (*Danse* 17).

King describes his first real encounter with horror at the age of four. He wanted to listen to a radio adaptation of Ray Bradbury's story "Mars Is Heaven" on the series *Dimension X*. His mother didn't want him to hear the story because he was too young, but he listened through the door. That night he was too frightened to sleep in his bed and slept where he could see the light from the bathroom (*Danse* 120–21). King also notes some of the literary influences from this period in his life. He always read a great deal. When the family returned to Durham, King was able to explore a relative's attic. He found a collection of his father's things including a reel of movie film and boxes of books, one of which contained an H. P. Lovecraft anthology of horror stories. "So that book, courtesy of my departed father, was my first taste of a world that went deeper than the B-pictures which played at the movies on Saturday afternoon" (*Danse* 101–2). Even though the books disappeared in a couple of weeks (King suspected a disapproving aunt), Lovecraft provided an introduction to the world of horror literature. King credits the *Ripley's Believe It or Not!* series of paperbacks published by Pocket Books with introducing him to the world of amazing facts. "It was in *Ripley's Believe It or Not!* that I first began to see how fine the line between the fabulous and the humdrum could sometimes be, and to understand that the juxtaposition of the two did as much to illuminate the ordinary aspects of life as it did to illuminate its occasional weird outbreaks" (*Nightmares* 3).

Films, too, were an important influence for the young King. He remembers seeing his first movie, *Creature from the Black Lagoon*, at a drive-in when he was about seven. King knew the creature was not real, but he also knew that a more realistic version would visit him at some point in his dreams (*Danse* 104). King sees this example of how children juggle their belief in the world of the imagination as the key to their openness. Adults have lost their ability to expose themselves to these possibilities. A successful horror film returns us to that childhood state where we can believe in the possibility that the monster exists (*Danse* 105–6). Even when King watches the same film twenty-two years later with his son he still has enough imagination for the film to have an effect on him (*Danse* 110).

While King believes that writers are made through hard work, he does describe other incidents from his childhood which had an effect on the direction of his work. He tells of dowsing with his Uncle Clayton. Once Uncle Clayt found the water he let King hold the dowsing stick, and King felt it move at the same spot. He compares talent to the water, which is there but must be developed (*Danse* 94–97).

King wrote his first horror story when he was seven. Later he got an old Underwood typewriter whose letters kept breaking. Like Paul Sheldon in *Misery*, he had to fill in some of the letters by hand. King began submitting stories to magazines when he was twelve (Winter, *Art* 18–19). He was also interested in real crime. He was fascinated with Carl Starkweather, who went on a murder spree across the country and kept a scrapbook of clippings. He both loved and was terrified of this real killer (Winter, *Art* 20).

The town of Durham was also important in King's early life. It is the basis for Derry, Castle Rock, 'salem's Lot, and all the other small Maine towns in his work. The Harmony Grove Cemetery becomes Harmony Hill in *'Salem's Lot*. A dead body he saw being pulled out of a lake reappears in the short story "The Body" in *Different Seasons*. King attended a one-room schoolhouse in Durham, another element of the image of the American Dream in his life. He graduated at the top of his class of three in the spring of 1962 (Beahm, *Stephen King Story* 29). King had a rather average high school experience. In his youth he was heavy and not very athletic, like his hero in *It*, Bill Denbrough. The town hired an old limousine to take the students to Lisbon High School in Lisbon Falls. One of the two young women who shared the limo became a model for Carrie. King generally got good grades, except in chemistry and physics, and played left tackle in football and rhythm guitar in a rock band. He was best known for his writing talent (Beahm, *Stephen King Story* 29). He published his first story, "I Was a Teenage Grave Robber," in a comics fan magazine, *Comics Review*, in 1965 (Winter, *Art* 22). He wrote his first full-length work, *The Aftermath*, during this period, but he was best known for a high school newspaper called *Village Vomit*, which once earned him a three-day suspension from school (Winter, *Art* 22).

## COLLEGE YEARS

During the summer of 1966, after graduating from high school, King started writing *Getting It On*, which he later published under the pseudonym Richard Bachman as *Rage*. This novel about an outsider who holds his high school class hostage is the first evidence of King's mature writing. He uses his own feeling of not fitting in to create an original expression of the high school experience. Even though he was accepted at Drew University, a Methodist college near New York City, King could not afford to go there, and went instead to the University of Maine in Orono. During his freshman year he sold his first story to a real magazine. *Startling Mystery Stories* published "The Glass Floor" (Winter, *Art* 23). While a freshman he also completed *The Long Walk*, which he later published as Richard Bachman. His professors were impressed with this novel. King submitted it to a competition and was crushed when it did not win (Beahm, *Stephen King Story* 40). The only other novel he completed during college was *Sword in the Darkness*, which has not been published.

King gained the most from his literature classes during his college years. He was strongly influenced by such naturalist writers as Thomas Hardy, Jack London, and Theodore Dreiser (Winter, *Art* 23). He also read a lot of popular fiction outside of the classroom. He felt that his creative writing classes actually inhibited him, but he greatly appreciated the support of his professors, who were very positive about his literary efforts. One helped him get an agent, but *Sword in the Darkness* never sold. He did publish several stories in *Ubris*, a college literary magazine. College also brought King in contact with new ideas. He entered the university a conservative, but the activism of colleges in the 1960s affected him. The student reaction to events in Vietnam changed his view of the world, and he joined in student protests. King saw horror fiction as an appropriate response to the times. He recognized that a film like *The Exorcist* was a parable for parents of how their children were being transformed into monsters (Beahm, *Stephen King Story* 46). He expressed his views on a variety of subjects in a column he wrote for the school newspaper, "King's Garbage Truck" (Winter, *Art* 25).

King had to work to support himself while at the university. In his senior year he had a job at the library, where he met his future wife, Tabitha Jane Spruce. While it was not love at first sight, they did date. Tabitha says she was more impressed with him than he was with her. She also describes King's extreme poverty at this time. "Talk about going to college poor—this guy was going to college the way people did in the twenties and thirties. He had nothing to eat, he had no money, he had no clothes; it was just incredible that anybody was going to school under those circumstances, and even more incredible that he didn't care" (Winter, *Art* 26). King began work on the first story in *The Dark Tower* series with one of the reams of colored paper that appeared in the library. But the story had to wait while King tried to find a job. He graduated on June 5, 1970, with a B.S. in English, a minor in speech, and a secondary school teaching certificate (Beahm, *Stephen King Story* 50). At the time there were not a lot of jobs for English teachers. King pumped gas and then worked in a laundry, which provided the background for his story "The Mangler." He also began writing stories for various men's magazines. *Cavalier*, in particular, published many of his horror stories.

## STRUGGLE AND FIRST SUCCESS

King struggled professionally, but his private life was going well. He married Tabitha on January 2, 1971, in Orono. Tabitha was Catholic, so the wedding was held at a Catholic church, but the reception was held at a Methodist church to give King's religion equal time (Beahm, *Stephen*

*King Story* 54). Tabitha graduated from the University of Maine in May 1971. She could not find a job in her field either, and worked as a waitress at a Dunkin' Donuts in Bangor, Maine (Beahm, *Stephen King Story* 55). King decided to try publishing *Getting It On,* his novel about high school. He sent it to Doubleday because they published so many books. He had also recently read *The Parallax View* by Loren Singer. He thought the editor of that book might be interested in his kind of writing. Singer's editor was sick when King's book arrived, and it was given to Bill Thompson, who liked the novel but couldn't persuade Doubleday to publish it. King was disappointed by this rejection. He took a teaching job at Hampden Academy, where he had done his student teaching, for $6,400 a year.

By this point the Kings had two children and were living in a trailer in Hermon, Maine. There was so little room that King wrote at a child's desk in the furnace room. They had little money. "Tabby juggled the bills with the competent but scary expertise of a circus clown juggling tennis racquets; the transmission on our senile 1965 Buick Special began to whine, then to groan, then to chug and hitch; and as winter came in, the snow-mobiles began to buzz across the fields" (Underwood and Miller, *Fear Itself* 19–20). King was desperate and didn't have any ideas. He had not thought of writing a horror novel, even though he had been selling horror stories. He decided to work on a short story he had begun the summer before called "Carrie" (Underwood and Miller, *Fear Itself* 20). King thought the opening scene in the women's shower unrealistic, so he threw the pages in the wastebasket. Luckily Tabitha retrieved them and urged him to continue. King persisted even when it looked like the work would be novella length—longer than a short story but shorter than a novel—which would make it unsellable (Underwood and Miller, *Fear Itself* 21–22).

In January 1973 King sent *Carrie* to Thompson at Doubleday. Thompson suggested some revisions, which King realized would strengthen the book. Thompson liked the rewrite, and in February King went to New York. A typical country hick, he bought a map and got blisters on his feet walking to the restaurant for lunch because he had new shoes. His neck was stiff from looking at the buildings. He had not slept on the bus and got drunk on two gin and tonics. "I had never been so determined to make no glaring social *gaffe* and never so convinced (at least since the night of my high school junior prom) that I would make one. To top off everything, I ordered fettucini, a dish bearded young men should avoid"

(Underwood and Miller, *Fear Itself* 25). Somehow King did not destroy his chances with this performance. A month later Tabitha used a neighbor's phone to call him at school with the news that Doubleday was going to publish *Carrie*. The publisher offered him an advance of $2,500, which was a good amount for a first novel. The Kings used the money to buy a new car. But the real money for *Carrie* came with the paperback sales.

King knew that the hardcover sales would not be good for a new author, especially for a horror story. Publishers tend to promote what they consider serious fiction in hardcover, especially when dealing with a first novel. Paperback publishers are more interested in popular fiction. *Carrie* attracted the attention of New American Library, which bid $400,000 for the paperback rights. According to its standard contract, Doubleday kept half of the money from the paperback sale of a novel. (This policy would later lead King to leave the publisher.) King couldn't believe the amount of the sale and had to call Thompson back. For the next few weeks, he was certain someone had made a mistake (Underwood and Miller, *Fear Itself* 28). During this period King worked on a suspense novel, one he didn't sell. He got the idea for his second novel during a dinner conversation with Tabitha and his friend Chris Chesley. King was teaching *Dracula*, and they discussed what would happen if the Count appeared in the twentieth century. While King was sure the FBI would find him right away, Chris and Tabitha suggested that he look more closely at some of the small towns around them (Underwood and Miller, *Fear Itself* 29). A vampire's actions could easily be concealed in these communities, which have little contact with the outside world. King also feels that teaching Thorton Wilder's play *Our Town* gave him additional insight into small town life which was helpful in creating the setting of *'Salem's Lot*. King finished this novel, originally called *Second Coming*, just before he learned about the paperback sale of *Carrie*. Thompson was concerned that King would be typecast as a horror writer, but King was not worried, knowing that was the kind of book he could write best.

Before *Carrie* was published King's mother died from cancer after a long illness in 1973. King presents one view of her death in "The Woman in the Room," published in *Night Shift*, his first collection of short stories, which he dedicated to her. His mother had encouraged King's writing and often struggled to give him the postage to mail out his short stories. She knew about the sale of *Carrie*, and he was able to give her a prepublication copy of the book, but never lived to see the success he has achieved. His greatest tribute to Ruth Pillsbury King is *Dolores Claiborne* (1993). This novel, also dedicated to her, is a beautiful examination of the life of a hard-working mother in Maine.

In his article "On Becoming a Brand Name" King explains that publishers like to be able to bounce back and forth between hardcover editions of one book and paperback versions of another because each creates new interest in the author (Underwood and Miller, *Fear Itself*). With the sale of *Carrie* King decided to leave teaching to become a full-time writer. He didn't want to leave his students and was considered a good teacher, but King had always wanted to be a writer. When *'Salem's Lot* was published in 1975 King was on his way to the major success he has achieved as an author.

After writing two books with Maine settings, King decided to live somewhere else for a while. The family moved to Boulder, Colorado, in the summer of 1974 and lived there for a year before returning to Maine (Beahm, *Stephen King Companion* 67). King tried to write a novel about the Patty Hearst kidnapping, but he could not develop the story. He and Tabitha decided to go away for a weekend and took the suggestion of friends to try the Stanley Hotel. They arrived the day before the hotel closed for the winter. They were the only guests, and King was inspired by what he saw at the hotel. He immediately began work on a book called *The Shine.* (The name was changed to *The Shining* when King learned that "shine" was a disparaging term applied to African Americans.) *The Shining* was the first King novel to become a hardcover best seller (Underwood and Miller, *Fear Itself* 41). With its publication King was well on his way to becoming a brand name, an author whose name would sell the book.

## THE SUCCESSFUL AUTHOR

King's rise to fame and fortune after hard work and rejection reaffirms our belief in the American Dream. While King's novels often explore the dark side of American life, he personally continues to embody much of what is considered best in this country. Unlike some people who grow up poor and suddenly become wealthy, King does not seem to have been spoiled by success. He continues to work just as hard after his early achievements. He still approaches his writing with discipline and works almost every day. "I take Christmas, my birthday, Easter and the Fourth of July off and write the other 361 days each year" (Underwood and

Miller, *Fear Itself* 37). He sets himself a goal for each day. "I work about two hours a day, but I work seven days a week. I write six pages a day, and that's like engraved in stone." If you divide the number of pages in the novel by six, you can tell how long it took him to write the book. He also rewrites as he goes along. On the second draft he fixes little things, "like taking a deck of cards and squaring them up so they're even" (Underwood and Miller, *Bare* 75). On the third draft he concentrates on the language. King wants his work to be accessible. "It should be like a good car. You have a good car and when the engine is in tune and running right, you can't hear the motor, but that doesn't mean it isn't doing its work" (Underwood and Miller, *Bare* 75). King likes to write to loud rock and roll music, which blocks out other sounds and helps him concentrate. He spends the rest of his workday dealing with other aspects of his career, such as giving interviews and answering fan mail.

King is realistic about his everyday life. He remains in Maine and is actively involved with his wife and three children, Naomi, Joe, and Owen. "You know, I've got three kids and I've changed all their diapers in the middle of the night, and when it's two o'clock in the morning and you're changing something that's sort of special delivery with one eye shut you don't *feel* famous" (Underwood and Miller, *Bare* 1). He also feels that staying in Maine has helped him keep a perspective on his life. "And I live in Bangor, Maine which is not a town calculated to make anybody feel famous. The only claim to fame is a big plastic statue of Paul Bunyan. You just live there and keep your head down" (Underwood and Miller, *Bare* 1–2). King is an avid baseball fan, and his team is the Boston Red Sox. He marks the year by the opening and closing of the baseball season, shaving his beard when the season opens and growing it again for the winter after the World Series.

During the 1980s King continued to publish regularly, and his fame increased. People also began to write books about him. His books were making so much money that he took a cash advance of only $1 for *Christine*. He felt that would free up advance money for less well known authors; it also meant he would receive royalties sooner (Beahm, *Stephen King Story* 108). His increased fame also led to discovery of his pseudonym. Some of his early unpublished novels, including *Rage* and *The Long Walk*, appeared under the name Richard Bachman because his publisher was afraid that too many novels appearing under King's name might hurt sales. When *Thinner* was published people began to notice stylistic similarities between King and Bachman, since *Thinner* was a recent creation and had more of King's mature style (Beahm, *Stephen King Story* 122–23).

Fame has advantages and disadvantages for King. He was on the October 6, 1985, cover of *Time* magazine, confirming his place in American popular culture (Beahm, *Stephen King Story* 133). King also tells about having dinner at a restaurant with one of his idols, Bruce Springsteen. A young woman dining with her family at a nearby table approached King and Springsteen. Springsteen took out a pen to sign an autograph. But she was interested in King and told him she had read every one of his books (Beahm, *Stephen King Story* 133). Some encounters with fans were not as positive. The Kings had to fence in their Bangor home and had to take even stronger security measures when a fan actually broke into the house and claimed to have a bomb. Tabitha was able to get out of the house, and the bomb was not real (Beahm, *Stephen King Story* 161).

The Kings have generously shared the benefits of success. King participates in many national charitable activities, but causes in Maine have benefited the most. The Kings have given money to the University of Maine-Orono swimming and diving programs and the Durham Elementary School for library books. They donated $750,000 in matching funds for the Old Town public library. Old Town, where Tabitha grew up, named a wing of the library in her honor. They also contributed matching funds to the Eastern Maine Medical Center for a pediatrics unit. Perhaps King's most visible contribution to the community is his donation of a million dollars for the construction of a 1,500-seat baseball park for Little League and Senior League teams in Bangor. Some residents call it "The Field of Screams" (Beahm, *Stephen King Companion* 189–90).

## FILMS

In *Danse Macabre* King devotes several chapters to horror films and acknowledges their influence on him and his work. He lists about a hundred fantasy/horror films and indicates his personal favorites. King also readily admits that films of his work have been important in contributing to his success. The film of *Carrie* did much to make people aware of this new author and boosted sales of that novel and *'Salem's Lot*, which followed it. King is not always happy with the film adaptations of his novels. And there are times when the public has agreed. While the quality of cinematic versions of his novels may vary, no film based on a work by King exactly reproduces the original. Films communicate visually, while novels use words. Often novels deal with the thoughts of the characters. Certain elements of the plot work better on paper than on the screen. Watching a film of a King work is never a substitute for reading his fiction.

King has viewed the films based on his novels with varying degrees of approval. While he is interested in what Stanley Kubrick did when he filmed *The Shining,* he feels that he and Kubrick had different opinions of what was important. With *The Lawnmower Man* he was angry that another story was grafted onto one of his short stories just to use his name. He took the production company to court and got his name removed from the film. King has worked on some of the adaptations of his films. He has written scripts, acted, and directed. His first acting experience was in one of the stories in *Creepshow,* an original screenplay of his. The director, George Romero, asked King to play Jordy Verrill in the segment entitled "The Lonesome Death of Jordy Verrill." King had the opportunity to direct his own work with the film *Maximum Overdrive.* While he enjoyed the process, he is not eager to direct another film. He found it to be too much like work, and it took too much time (Underwood and Miller, *Feast of Fear* 261).

Public reception of films adapted from King's work has varied with the quality of the film. Many nonfans have been surprised at some of the films. People associate King with supernatural horror. Rob Reiner's *Stand By Me,* a moving tale about boys growing up based on the story "The Body," found an audience beyond King's usual fans. *Misery,* Reiner's second King film, interested a similar audience and won an Academy Award for its star, Kathy Bates. Reiner named his production company Castle Rock Entertainment, after King's fictional town. Recently *The Shawshank Redemption,* which many feel failed to make money because of its title, also surprised people when they learned that its source was the King story "Rita Hayworth and the Shawshank Redemption," from *Different Seasons.* This film and *Dolores Claiborne* may suffer at the box office because they disappoint King fans looking for horror and fail to attract an audience put off by the King connection. King's work has also found its way to television with varying degrees of success. *'Salem's Lot* was an early television adaptation. In the last few years both *The Stand* and *The Langoliers,* published in *Four Past Midnight,* have appeared to bolster network standings during ratings weeks. While King remains concerned about how his name is used in adaptations, his works will continue to be adapted as long as there is public interest in them.

## KING'S STYLE AND THE FUTURE

While the subjects King deals with in his fiction change, his approach to his writing remains consistent. His style has developed and matured, but he still writes because he has stories he has to tell. He also wants to tell them a certain way. King has always believed in the importance of the story. "The stories themselves may be unbelievable. But within the framework of the stories I'm concerned that what people do in these stories should be as real as possible and that the characters of the people should be as real as possible" (Underwood and Miller, *Feast of Fear* 232). King concentrates on what he knows and has experienced, and finds it difficult to write about something outside of his experience. For example, he found it hard to write a scene in *Cujo* where a couple discusses the affair the wife is having (Underwood and Miller, *Feast of Fear* 234–35). But King also believes that he must do difficult things to maintain his artistic integrity. At the same time he is aware that his strength comes from working within his own experience. "The people who I write about are generally speaking not very rich or very cultured, maybe because I'm not very cultured, because I don't have any idea what it is to be rich . . . like estates in Newport . . . or having portraits in the hall" (Underwood and Miller, *Feast of Fear* 235–36).

King retains his fears of the monsters that may live under the bed, but includes fewer of them in his recent work. Because his children are grown, he finds himself less interested in childhood and he has dealt with more mature adults in most of his recent fiction. Certain projects continue to develop themes he began in his college days. *The Dark Tower* is an ongoing series, and its themes also appear in novels like *Insomnia* and *Rose Madder*. He is also dealing more seriously with themes which have been a smaller part of his work, such as aging and wife and child abuse.

One of the most notable aspects of King's development as a writer has been his ability to continue to grow. He has not let fame force him into repeating patterns which are proven successes. He has never been afraid to go against critical opinion. He knows that many critics dismiss him because they do not know how to deal seriously with authors who write popular fiction. He does not write to please his critics. But recently he has been willing to write novels which may surprise his fans. Some of his short fiction does not feature the supernatural. *Cujo* deals with realistic horror. *Rose Madder* (1995) employs the supernatural in a traditional manner but one King has not previously used. *Dolores Claiborne,* aside from brief telepathic moments, is a realistic novel. *Insomnia* has interesting connections with *The Dark Tower* series. All of these novels are examples of the way King continues to explore and enlarge his fictional world. He does not know how his work will stand up in the future. He thinks it will still be in libraries if we still have libraries. He knows the test of a writer is how long his work is around after his death. "After I'm dead some eleven year old kid will be going along through the stacks the way I went through the library stacks and discovered Richard Matheson and Algernon Blackwood, and he'll find this dusty book and he'll take it home and he'll lose an afternoon" (Underwood and Miller, *Feast of Fear* 238). Charles Dickens was the most popular writer of his time. Now he is a classroom assignment. King's view of his future is a little more hopeful. Maybe it's better to be picked up off a shelf by chance than to be assigned in an English class.

Everyone who reads King's work has favorites. While I like some of his novels better than others, I have varying reasons for choosing the novels featured in this work. I have tried to show the variety of King's work and at the same time have concentrated on his most recent work. I felt it important to explore the development of his style and themes. *'Salem's Lot* and *The Shining* are early examples of how King deals with such traditional forms as the vampire and ghost story. *The Stand* is King's most ambitious novel and has recently been reissued in an uncut edition. In *The Dark Half* King examines both the role of the author and the connection between mystery and horror. *The Waste Lands* is the third volume in *The Dark Tower* series. King has begun to connect elements of this series to the rest of his fiction. *Needful Things* marks the end of King's use of the town of Castle Rock, the imaginary site of both novels and short stories. *Dolores Claiborne, Insomnia,* and *Rose Madder,* King's most recent novels, are examples of new directions in his fiction. I have attempted to connect the rest of King's fiction to these novels. If I have omitted one of your favorites, I hope I may have introduced you to one you have overlooked.

# 2

# Genre

## WHAT IS A GENRE?

When you choose what you read because you expect it to treat a topic in a certain way, you are usually making decisions based on your experience with a literary genre. One way to group fiction works is by genre. In a bookstore you expect the mystery shelves to contain books dealing with crimes and their solutions. If you look at the section on romance you know you will find books which concentrate on love relationships. The science fiction section contains books dealing with the future. The separation of fiction into different genres is a way of focusing the reader's expectations and the author's creativity. The categories allow readers to select literature they like and avoid categories they may not like. If horror fiction frightens you, you avoid that section of the bookstore. Similarly, authors may be interested in dealing with a certain way of looking at the world. If they like to create other worlds, they might choose to write in the fantasy or science fiction genre.

Works of nonfiction can also be categorized by genre. History and biography are examples of nonfiction genres. Fiction and nonfiction are opposites and generally deal with their subjects in different ways. For example, biography concentrates on the life of a person, and history deals with public events; both are based on factual information. Fiction may concentrate on people or events, but it need not rely on actual facts to tell its story. The differences among fictional genres such as horror, fantasy, and science fiction are less clear. Although readers and authors may not always agree on where to place a book, they agree that the categories do exist. Even if you are not very familiar with a category you still may have a good idea of what belongs in it. People who don't read horror novels may say, "I don't read that kind of book," and be able to give reasons why they don't like the genre.

Genres develop over time, reflecting shifts in literary styles and tastes. Genres reflect the society around them, but do more than mirror the world. They may show us our fears about our lives and about both our personal future and the future of the planet.

We may disagree about which works belong in each category because genres do not remain static. Each uses narrative, motive, setting, characterization, and symbolism to create its own fictional world. We may also stress distinct elements in a genre. Take, for example, a story with a western setting that takes place in the future. If we feel that setting is the most important aspect of the genre, we would characterize it as a western rather than science fiction. The author, however, might think that the time frame is more important, and call it science fiction. We cannot make a definitive list of the basics of a genre, but we can describe the elements that characterize it. Much of our pleasure in experiencing a genre comes from our anticipation of meeting the familiar and expected in a new form.

## WHAT IS THE HORROR GENRE?

Most people think of Stephen King as someone who writes horror fiction. But before we can discuss his specific approach to this genre, we need to understand its components. Some authors and critics are interested in the way horror relates to its audience. Most people read horror fiction or see horror films because they like the kinds of reactions this genre stimulates in them. King wants you to be scared by his work. Some of us read horror fiction as a way of testing ourselves; we can come near death without dying. It's like getting on the most frightening ride in the amusement park. We can see how brave we are without actually risking our lives.

Many people define horror by its subjects. We all think of creatures like Frankenstein's monster, Dracula, and the wolfman as monsters in the horror genre. Each one of these creatures has a history and developed over a period of time. But we also know that horror covers more than just these monsters. We could all make long lists of the kind of creatures we identify with horror, especially when we think of films as well as literature. The minute we would start to make such a list we would also realize that not all monsters are alike and that not all horror deals with monsters. The subject approach is not the clearest way to define this genre.

Some students of this genre find that the best way to examine it is to deal with the way horror fiction is organized or structured. Examining the organization of a horror story shows that it shares certain traits with other types of fiction. Horror stories share the use of suspense as a tactic with many other kinds of literature. The tension we feel when a character goes into the attic, down into the basement, or just into the abandoned house is partially a result of suspense. We don't know what is going to happen. But that suspense is intensified by our knowledge of the genre. We know that characters involved in the world of horror always meet something awful when they go where they shouldn't. Part of the tension is created because they are doing something we know is going to get them in trouble. Stephen King refers directly to our anticipation of horror. In *'Salem's Lot* Susan approaches the house which is the source of evil. "She found herself thinking of those drive-in horror movie epics where the heroine goes venturing up the narrow attic stairs . . . or down into some dark, cobwebby cellar . . . and she . . . thinking: *What a silly bitch . . . I'd never do that!*" (260). Of course Susan's fears are justified. She does end up dead in the basement, a victim of the vampire.

If the horror genre uses the character's search for information to create suspense, it controls when and where we get our knowledge. Because we are outside of the situation we usually know more than the characters. Our advance knowledge creates suspense because we can anticipate what is going to happen. The author can play with those expectations by either confirming them or surprising us with a different outcome. When suspense is an important element in fiction we may often find that the plot is the most critical part of the story. We care more about what happens next than about who the characters are or where the story is set. But setting is often considered a part of the horror genre. If the genre has traditional monsters, it also has traditional settings. Only authors who want to challenge the tradition place events in bright, beautiful parks. We expect a connection between the setting and the events in this genre. We are not surprised to find old houses, abandoned castles, damp cellars, or dark forests as important elements in the horror story.

Some people make further distinctions based on how the stories are organized. We can divide stories into different categories based on how we come to believe in the events related and how they are explained to us. Stories that deal with parallel worlds expect us to accept those worlds without question. We just believe Dorothy is in Oz; we accept Oz as a parallel world separate from ours. Other times events seem to be supernatural but turn out to have natural explanations: the ghosts turn out to be squirrels in the attic, or things that move mysteriously are part of a plot to drive someone crazy. Sometimes the supernatural is the result of the way the central character sees the world, as in stories told from the point of view of a crazy person. But at times we are not sure, and hesitate about believing in the possibility of the supernatural. When I first read *Dracula* I seriously considered hanging garlic on my windows because I believed that vampires could exist. This type of hesitation, when we almost believe, falls into the general category of the "fantastic" (Todorov 25). Often horror has its greatest effect on us because we almost believe, or believe while we are reading the book or watching the film, that the events are possible.

Yet another way of categorizing works of horror is by the source of the horror. Some horror comes from inside the characters. Something goes wrong inside, and a person turns into a monster. Dr. Frankenstein's need for knowledge turns him into the kind of person who creates a monster. Dr. Jekyll also values his desire for information above all else, and creates Mr. Hyde. In another kind of horror story the threat to the central character or characters comes from outside. An outside force may invade the character and then force the evil out again. The vampire attacks the victim, but then the victim becomes a vampire and attacks others. Stories of ghosts or demonic possession also fall into this category.

We can also look at the kinds of themes common to horror. Many works concentrate on the conflict between good and evil. Works about the fantastic may deal with the search for forbidden knowledge that appears in much horror literature. Such quests are used as a way of examining our attitude toward knowledge. While society may believe that new knowledge is always good, the horror genre may question this assumption, examining how such advances affect the individual and society.

Modern horror fiction begins with Gothic fiction. Horace Walpole's

*The Castle of Otranto* (1764) is the first real Gothic novel, the first of many to deal with heroines in jeopardy, rotting castles and monasteries, and natural and supernatural events combined to create sensational suspense. Much of the supernatural threat comes from outside the character. At this period people were just beginning to question the relationship between the world of science and the world of religion. Scientific advances gave rational explanations for many events previously thought to have supernatural or religious sources. This conflict between the world of science and the world of belief is reflected in Gothic literature as it developed over the eighteenth and nineteenth centuries. The story of Dr. Frankenstein's experiments to create life reflects society's concerns with the role of science. The Gothic novel generally reflects concerns about advances in knowledge and whether they will be good or bad for society.

As the horror genre developed, the idea of threats from the inside grew. For many people religion lost its power as a source of supernatural events. Horror had to be believable within a world where more and more could be explained rationally. While the genre still kept its connection to the more general concerns of society, the source of the horror was more personal. In King's *Christine*, for example, the car turns into a destructive monster because it is bought and restored by a teenager who fails to fit into his social group. Religion, too, has lost much of its power in this novel. The car is destroyed without the use of religious objects. But the modern horror novel is still concerned with the search for knowledge and how it affects our world. Modern science and technology are often sources for evil. In *Firestarter* a child's powers are the result of experiments on her parents. We might even think of science as a substitute for religion in many modern horror stories. In the Gothic story, we accept devils and evil monks as integral parts of the world of the priests, crosses, and holy water by means of which the evil is destroyed. Now we believe in the power of science to create the new monsters of modern horror and also to help us control them.

## KING'S VIEW OF THE HORROR GENRE

King describes his view of the genre and lists his favorite literature and film in *Danse Macabre* (1981). A critic, Tony Magistrale, analyzes the points King makes about modern horror in this work (*Stephen King, The Second Decade* 21–24). All of his points deal with our relationship with modern horror media, including film and television as well as literature. We will look at how these points relate directly to King's work.

Magistrale's first point is that horror *"allows us to prove our bravery"* (22). Many people see this as an important element in the genre. We can test ourselves without really facing physical danger. We can assure ourselves that we might respond heroically in the same situation, or we can face our fears by continuing to read, even though we are frightened. King relates these experiences to teenagers' love of the horror genre and the amusement park. People who hold their hands in the air on the roller-coaster are testing their bravery in the same way people do when they read a scary story or watch a frightening film.

Second, horror *"enables us to reestablish feelings of normality"* (22). Horror allows us to see that our own world is not as bad as the world of the novel. We may not like high school, but our lives are certainly better than those of the central characters in *Carrie* or *Christine*. We may miss our dead loved ones, but they have not come back like the family in *Pet Sematary*. Our childhood may have been unhappy, but we have not lost our brother to a monster, as Bill Denbrough did in *It*. And our insomnia is nothing compared to the sleeplessness of the characters in the book of that title.

Magistrale's third point may become less valid as King's work develops: *"It confirms our good feelings about the status quo"* (22). King suggests that the horror genre appeals to the conservative because it shows us how bad things might be. The other worlds of the horror novel make us think our own world isn't that bad. But many of King's recent novels show worlds that are very close to our own. In *Dolores Claiborne* and *Insomnia* average humans make the world a better place. And both novels explore themes of current concern, such as child and wife abuse and abortion rights.

The fourth point may suggest why King may be moving toward novels which give us ways to deal with social problems: *"It lets us feel we are part of the larger whole"* (22). In *It* we identify with the group that has come together to finally destroy the horror which has been a part of the town for a long time. Even if they are not all working together, we also identify with the people who work against the alien evil of *The Tommyknockers*. In *The Stand* King examines the benefits and risks of forming groups. He also looks at the family as a group and usually feels that we are better off with groups we form on our own.

The fifth point is central to the horror genre: *"It provides an opportunity to penetrate the mystery of death"* (22). We don't often deal with our concerns about death in everyday life. A novel like *Pet Sematary* shows one way of coping with the death of loved ones. We also get some sense of possible versions of life after death in this novel, *It,* and *The Tommyknockers. Insomnia* explores the complex relationship between our world and the world beyond death. We can also identify with a character who is trying to avoid death. In *Cujo* a mother is trapped in her car with her child and has to face the possibility of death from a rabid dog. Facing death goes beyond just testing our bravery. The young boy in *The Cycle of the Werewolf* is willing to sacrifice to rid his town of the murderer. Horror may even suggest what might happen beyond death. We also see how characters may be willing to die to save others.

If death is a major focus of the horror genre, the sixth point connects our fears to a larger concern: *"It permits us to indulge our darkest collective and social anxieties"* (23). The genre gives us ways to deal with some of our fears about the world. In *The Dead Zone* the central character's powers give him knowledge about destructive political forces. Both *Carrie* and *Christine* examine our concerns about what happens to the outsider in high school. We can then go deeper, to a subtext which connects the world of high school to society as a whole. The genre gives us ways of examining the larger problems facing society. This point also connects to the earlier points about the way the genre deals with the effects of science and technology in our lives.

The seventh point is a major element in many of King's novels: *"It lets us return to childhood"* (23). Often children provide the key to our understanding of the world of horror. They see clearly because they have not yet learned the adult habits of disbelief. Adults must return to their childhood if they are to survive in King's world of horror. Or they must finally confront their childhood terrors. Parents are usually trying too hard to be adults to connect with their children and accept their view of the world. Only the exceptional adult who has not totally lost contact with the world of childhood can see into the horror in King's novels. Children do not have to be convinced; they believe what they see. They also have an innocence and goodness often lost in the adult. The characters in *It* confront the evil twice. The first time they succeed because they are children. The second time, as adults, they must confront their childhood fears in order to finally conquer the horror. Many of King's adults can defeat the evils in the genre only after they deal with their childhood fears. To survive, the heroine of *Gerald's Game* must deal with the moment of child abuse she experienced. Many of the elements of the horror genre come from our childhood fears. The horrible things which can happen in the dark, terrifying strangers, the monsters who live in the closet and under the bed are all elements of the genre. We return to the world of childhood when we accept the possibility that these things may still exist. Those of us with enough imagination to get up and close the closet door so that we can sleep are still close to our childhood. We are the ones who most often deal with evil in King's world, and, as readers, we are the ones who respond to this world.

The final point in the list returns us to our everyday world: *"It enables us to transcend the world of darkness and negation"* (23). King suggests that we leave our experience with the genre with skills which allow us to cope with the evil we find in our own lives. As we identify with those who are tested, we see what is important for our own survival. We learn that we must confront our fears and believe in the power of good in our lives. We can also see that our problems are not that difficult when we watch characters master much greater conflicts. Horror also allows us to return to the world of our childhood. If we regain its fears, we also regain its beliefs.

Many people think that an interest in horror is unhealthy. They see the monsters, the evil, the darkness. King wants people to realize that the genre moves us through horror to a world where basic human values have been tested and reaffirmed. The world at the end of one of his novels is not the same as at the beginning. Towns may be destroyed, some people may have died, but others have been tested and have survived. The few who do succeed in overcoming evil face a world which has been cleansed. We have hope for our own world. Whatever may happen, good can win, and we have learned how to work toward the defeat of evil in our own world.

## OTHER GENRES IN KING'S FICTION

We tend to think of King as a writer of horror fiction, but not all of his work falls directly into this category. Some combines horror with other genres. *Carrie* is set a few years in the future, but we read it as a horror novel. The setting is only a way of making the story more real. If we haven't heard of Carrie's powers, it is because the story hasn't happened yet. Other novels are clearly part of other genres.

## Suspense Fiction

The suspense genre shares much of its structure with horror. Both encourage identification with the central character or characters. And both use the plot and the reader's expectations to create tension. If we know more than the characters we can anticipate what might happen. If we share the viewpoint of the character, we identify with that character. While in horror the source of the tension may be supernatural, in suspense its source is the natural world. In *Misery* an author is trapped in the house of his biggest fan. We identify with him and his attempts to escape and outwit his captor. The woman who has trapped him may be crazy, but there are natural causes for her mental state. In *Gerald's Game* a woman is trapped. A visitor seems to be supernatural, but we find out that he too has a natural origin. *Cujo* is a real dog who suffers from rabies. We may be able to read his thoughts, but we see this as King creating a personality for him rather than a supernatural communication.

In other novels King gives logical reasons for events that appear to have supernatural causes. In *The Dead Zone* and *Firestarter* characters' powers have logical origins. Such things could happen, but have not happened in our world. Some events in suspense novels we already know to be possible—people have been attacked by rabid dogs or crazy fans. But other events require us to accept the unlikely—we do not know of people who have started fires with their minds.

## Science Fiction

Science fiction novels explore events in the future. The characters face problems in a world of the future. Science fiction may also deal with problems created by worlds other than our own. *The Stand* examines the difficulties facing the survivors of a strange epidemic. The central characters in *The Tommyknockers* uncover an alien spacecraft. As the craft is revealed, strange things happen to people near it. *The Dark Tower* series also deals with an unspecified future. In these novels characters travel in time, another trait of the science fiction genre. Science fiction creates uncertainty just as horror and suspense do. But in this genre we are interested in how events work out in the future or in other worlds. Science fiction uses myths and symbols to help create its world, and its picture of the future may be critical of the present. For example, *The*

*Talisman*, which King wrote with Peter Straub, deals with concern about the effects of nuclear power on our future.

## Fantasy

The fantasy genre is closely related to both horror and science fiction. Fantasy explores supernatural events. But these events do not happen in our world, and the author does not try to make them seem realistic. Fantasy literature is usually set in an alternate parallel world in a mythical past. Fantasy also shares certain traits with the fairy tale. Fairy tales occur in a mythical world and focus on supernatural or magical events. Many of King's novels have connections to popular fairy tales. The prom at the end of *Carrie* recalls elements of Cinderella. Jack in *The Shining* becomes Bluebeard. Children, who are so important in King's horror fiction, are the intended audience for fairy tales. Like science fiction, fantasy explores parallel or alternate worlds. While science fiction may deal with alien universes, fantasy locates its world in a different reality which is still connected to our planet.

*The Eyes of the Dragon* is King's major exploration of the fantasy genre. He wrote the book for his daughter because she didn't like horror. This novel deals with two brothers, an evil wizard, and magical events. Even the illustrations add to the fantasy and the sense of an undefined past. The opening page looks like an illuminated manuscript, and each chapter begins with a letter in a special typeface. Even though there is much tension in the story, we are drawn along by events the way we might be in a fairy tale. And even though terrible things may happen, we know that the fairy tale must have a happy ending. We have faith that good magic will win over bad. But even in this novel there is a hint of evil which goes beyond the boundaries of any genre. Evil in this novel is represented by a man called Flagg. Flagg reappears in other forms in other King novels and as himself in *The Stand*. In King's world, where religion is no longer a power, Flagg becomes a kind of Satan, an evil figure who escapes to reappear later in another world or with another name. "Flagg always showed up with a different face and a different bag of tricks, but two things about him were always the same. He always came hooded, a man who seemed almost to have no face, and he never came as the King himself, but always as the whisperer in the shadows, the man who poured poison into the porches of the Kings' ears" (62).

King's use of Flagg is just one element that unites his work. He explores related genres with characters who share many traits. Even though his main emphasis is on the horror genre, his themes are remarkably consistent.

# 3

# *'Salem's Lot*
## (1975)

In *'Salem's Lot,* his second novel, Stephen King turns to the horror tradition for his inspiration. Carrie, the heroine of his first novel, is possessed by rare supernatural powers which allow her to move objects through space. Ben Mears, the adult hero of *'Salem's Lot,* must use his human skills and the knowledge of the vampire tradition supplied by his young friend Mark Petrie to defeat the vampires in this novel. As his writing career develops, King creates more characters who are ordinary people in unusual situations, in contrast to heroes or heroines whose personalities are controlled by the supernatural.

King develops a narrative pattern in *'Salem's Lot* which he will explore through much of his career, using a prologue and an epilogue to frame the story. After the prologue he introduces his central character and the town and the people who live there. The town of Jerusalem's Lot, often shortened to 'salem's Lot, is an important character in the novel. It is the kind of place which may seem ordinary on the surface but which can hide terrible secrets, one of the small Maine towns that has fascinated King throughout his career.

In *'Salem's Lot* Ben Mears returns to the town where he spent four years of his childhood to write a new novel. He immediately meets people who become important in his personal life and in the job of dealing with the evil which has also come to the town. Ben is drawn to the Marsten House, where he had a frightening experience as a child. For initiation into a club, nine-year-old Ben had to go into the deserted house and bring something back. When he went upstairs and opened a door he saw the ghost of Hubie Marsten, who had hanged himself in that room. Ben ran out of the house still holding the glass snow globe he had picked up from the table in the front hall. The adult Ben thinks he would like to rent the house, but when he looks up at it with Susan Norton, a young woman he has met, there is a light in a window. They later learn that the partners who have bought the house are even more evil than Hubie Marsten, a bootlegger who shot his wife and committed suicide.

Richard Throckett Straker has purchased the house for his partner, Mr. Barlow. He also buys a laundromat, which he turns into an antique shop. Gradually, Ben begins to suspect that the strange disappearances and deaths in 'salem's Lot are connected to Straker, Barlow, and the Marsten House. A small group of people who begin to share his beliefs come together to destroy the evil. This confrontation of a small group with an evil force which threatens society is at the heart of *'Salem's Lot*.

## PLOT DEVELOPMENT AND NARRATIVE POINT OF VIEW

A writer can choose many ways to tell a story. The author may narrate it as if she or he is a character experiencing the events: "I am telling you what happened to me or what I saw." This is known as the first person point of view, and the reader can only know what that character experiences. Sometimes an author tells the story from a specific character's point of view: "He saw her walking down the street." This kind of storytelling uses the third person point of view, and, again, we can only know what that character experiences. When the author moves to another character, our information then becomes limited to that person's knowledge. An author can also tell the story without limiting what we know to certain characters. This approach is called the "omniscient" or "all-knowing" point of view. King usually uses the third person point of view in the body of the novel, but the prologue and epilogue of *'Salem's Lot* are presented by an all-knowing narrator.

"Almost everyone thought the man and the boy were father and son" (xi). This sentence, which stands alone as the first paragraph of the novel, suggests that these two characters are not related by blood ties. At the same time the sentence suggests the importance of any kind of father/

son connection, not just a blood relationship. King opens up questions for the reader by not giving the characters' names immediately. Later, in the main body of the novel, we learn the characters' names: Ben Mears is the man, and Mark Petrie the boy. But the use of "boy" and "man" also creates a connection between the words which is central to Ben Mears's quest and to Mark Petrie's ultimate salvation. If Ben returns to 'salem's Lot to finally deal with his childhood fears, Mark must continue to see and think like a child, but he has to make adult decisions.

The second paragraph of the novel is filled with details about the cross-country journey of these two unnamed characters. We meet them in the middle of their journey. We get a few clues about the man. He is tall, with black hair, and is surprised at his success as an auto mechanic in a temporary job he takes. The mass of detail presents a problem. We don't know which points will be important later in the novel. Like the old joke where we try to keep track of the number of people getting on and off the bus when we were really *supposed* to count the number of stops, we don't know what we need to remember. The pair finally stops in a small California town near the border.

The man buys newspapers and looks for information about Jerusalem's Lot. King teases the reader with references to unspeakable events taking place in this small town throughout the prologue without ever telling exactly what has happened. He creates uneasiness about both the facts he presents and their future meaning. Gradually a pattern emerges from the mass of details. The man is a novelist who completes and sells a new book. The boy is intelligent, troubled, and very attached to the man. The boy refuses to look at the newspapers or talk about Jerusalem's Lot, and he has nightmares. At the end of the first chapter of the prologue, the novel is sold. "The man quit his job at the gas station, and he and the boy crossed the border" (xii). King casually draws attention to the idea of borders, which will become one of the novel's themes. The border is not a separation between two countries. It is a further retreat from the horror the man and the boy have experienced, which the reader has only begun to anticipate.

We get additional details from a newspaper issue in which the man's name is mentioned. "It was not over in 'salem's Lot yet it seemed" (xiii). The boy does read this article; they share their fears. The newspaper deals with how Jerusalem's Lot has become a ghost town. Even though the man's name is in the article, it is not included in the section we read. The boy's family is mentioned, but not his first name. Of course, we can only see these differences when we reread the novel. King gives important clues, but not enough information for us to pick out the important details.

The article is followed by the boy's entry into the church and his confession. King builds suspense by not letting us know what the boy confesses. When the priest talks to the man, we are even more interested in the contents of the confession. The priest says that he has never heard such a strange confession. Finally the man and the boy agree that they must return to 'salem's Lot. The end of the prologue describes the man's thoughts as he begins to remember Jerusalem's Lot. King connects his memories with a snowball glass paperweight, continuing the pattern of teasing his readers. Just when we think we are finally going to get answers about 'salem's Lot, King introduces another piece of the puzzle. The prologue can be seen as the movement of two of the characters to the decision to return to 'salem's Lot. But the reader must deal with a mass of detail and many questions. The boy's acceptance of religion suggests a power which helps him return to his past, but we have only our belief in King as storyteller to guide us on our journey through the novel.

The man and the boy already know all there is to know about their journey. They travel to bring an end to events. But the reader has only vague ideas of their goals. And the reader moves from their decision to return to yet another journey in the first chapter of the main novel where, once again, King presents many facts, including a name, Ben Mears, a date, September 5, 1975, and a location, the Maine turnpike. We may remember that the newspaper article from the prologue talked about events in 'salem's Lot taking place after the 1970 census. We may be confused about the time, but we have an important clue that the main body of the novel must take place before the events in the prologue.

Suddenly we are plunged into a third person point of view narration with a character in a conversation with himself. Like the unnamed characters of the prologue, we learn that Mears is returning to 'salem's Lot to deal with an episode from his past. As he enters the town he stops to look at a strange, evil building, the Marsten House, which overlooks the landscape. We learn that he is haunted by the house, but King waits to tell us more about its history. Instead we meet some of the people who live in the town. Some of them will be central to the novel; others give information but remain in the background. Ben meets Susan Norton, who is sitting in a park reading one of his novels. We are now sure that Ben is the unnamed novelist of the prologue. King also lets us guess that the relationship between Ben and Susan will be important.

King moves back and forth from his introduction of the romance between these two people to his role as the all-knowing narrator who informs us of the history of the house and the discovery of the murder/suicide of its owners, Birdie and Hubie Marsten. Ben tells Susan about his own experience in the house. Once he establishes these facts, King introduces new characters. King never lets us relax completely. We may enjoy watching these two people fall in love, but King always undercuts their happiness with suggestions of something evil beneath the calm surface. He follows this same pattern when he introduces other townspeople. Again we do not know how important these people will be. As in the prologue, King keeps us off balance by not letting us know how to read these details.

King also introduces items which will become important only at the end of the story. We learn that Susan was born the year of the fire which was the biggest thing to ever happen to the town. Ben's aunt's house burned down, and he was sent back to his mother. We also learn of a memory which haunts Ben. While driving a motorcycle, he had an accident in which his wife, Miranda, was killed. King also tells us the town's population, 1,300. All these facts have a place in the story. King continues the patterns he sets up in the opening chapters throughout the novel, controlling important information as one way to keep us in suspense. He reveals just enough to help us connect some of the clues and figure out what is happening in 'salem's Lot. Aside from a few details from the past, such as Ben's experience in the Marsten House or Straker buying it, the events of the story are told in chronological order.

King also creates suspense by moving from character to character at key moments. He introduces Sandy McDougall; just as she hits her baby, he shifts to Mike Ryerson going to work. Mike, who keeps up the town's cemeteries, discovers a dog hanging on the spiked gate of one of them. King then introduces a school bus driver, lodgers at a boarding house, and, finally, Mark Petrie. King returns to some of these people only when they become vampires.

While King delays the introduction of Barlow, the vampire, until late in the story, he gives us clues to the strange events which begin to happen. We may not yet know who or what is important. But because we are introduced to everyone who plays a role in the story, we can put the pieces together faster than the characters can. We also have a good idea of what is going to happen before they do, which increases the suspense. Some characters have roles only as the vampires' victims, but others contribute to the fight against the vampires. Those who become vampires are typical members of a small community. King wants us to understand how effective a vampire can be in a place where we think nothing ever happens. We meet Hal and Jack Griffin doing their chores. We learn a lot about Eva Miller, who owns a boarding house, and some of the people who live there. We see Charlie Rhodes drive his school bus, and we meet Matthew Burke, a teacher.

Mark Petrie is one of the few characters to be introduced through action. We watch him beat the school bully. King wants us to believe that Mark is capable of the kind of actions he will take as the novel progresses. When we meet Danny and Ralph Glick we think we are dealing with just another introduction as the two boys set off through the woods to Mark's house. They tell their parents that they are going to look at Mark's electric trains. Ralph forces his older brother to take him by threatening to tell their parents the real reason for the trip. Mark has a complete collection of Aurora plastic monsters, and the brothers know that their parents would not approve of their looking at these gory figures. We get a little worried when Danny's teasing of his brother takes the form of tales of the deaths of small children. They sense something in the woods. Danny thinks not of ghosts but of "preeverts," but we're afraid the source of evil may be supernatural. Ralph disappears, and Danny can't give a good explanation of what happened to his brother.

King lets us know where Ralph is in a very short chapter that begins at 11:59 P.M. We are certain that bad things happen at midnight. King takes us back to the Harmony Hill Cemetery, but there is more than a dead dog waiting. A man whose voice may remind us of Straker calls for a sign from his lord. He brings a sacrifice, which we know is the body of Ralph. A silent wind rises up, and the figure stands with the body he is bringing his master. The last line is terrifying. "It became unspeakable" (73). We are not sure exactly what has happened, but we know it is awful. When the town responds to Ralph's disappearance with the usual search for a missing person, we know they will not succeed.

King slowly introduces more of the supernatural into the story. Straker has Larry Crockett, the real estate agent who sold him the Marsten House, hire two men to pick up some boxes from the Custom House Wharf in Portland, Maine. We know it is not going to be just another delivery when Straker gives the details of how they are to take a valuable sideboard to the Marsten House. They are to leave this box in the cellar and carefully padlock all of the doors. Royal Snow and Hank Peters find this special box very heavy. Something in it seems strange to Hank; also, it has no customs stamp even though it has come from London, England.

When they arrive at the house they don't want to take the box into the basement. When Hank has to go back into the cellar to place the key ring on the table, he sees what look like Ralph's shirt and jeans. One of the aluminum bands around the box snaps, and Hank runs out of the cellar.

A strange man visits Dud Rogers, who takes care of the dump. The stranger loves the predators of the night. Finally the stranger approaches Dud and gives him what King describes as sweet pain. King is still not specific, but we have a good idea that we have just met Barlow, who is tasting a victim. King then introduces the priest, Father Donald Callahan, who has been drinking not blood, but alcohol. The association of these two men presents the traditional conflict in a vampire novel between evil and religion.

The vampire begins to attack the town. Gradually its inhabitants feel ill. Mike, the grave digger, tells Matt about his symptoms. Mike can only sleep during the day, and he found his bedroom window open even though he had closed it. Matt offers Mike a bed at his house because the man is so frightened. Matt is terrified at the noises coming out of Mike's room during the night, especially the sucking sounds, and is the first to suspect vampire attacks. We see that he is convinced when he asks Ben to bring a crucifix. Mike is dead even though he looks like he is sleeping, but there are no marks on his neck. Matt says that the marks disappear when the victim dies. Ben agrees because he remembers both the Bram Stoker book and the film *Dracula*. At mention of these names the reader is certain that there are vampires in 'salem's Lot.

King takes a long time to get to the final recognition of the vampires operating in the town. He wants to take us slowly to the point where we will believe in the possibility that they might exist in the world of this novel. Once he establishes their existence the novel moves quickly. We watch the growth of the vampire community and the efforts of the small group of vampire hunters to stop the spread of this contagion. After Matt convinces Ben of the existence of the vampires, they are joined by Jimmy Cody, Father Callahan, Mark Petrie, and Susan. The hunters know they must deal with Barlow. When Susan goes to Marsten House she meets Mark, who is also investigating. They are both caught, but only Mark escapes. Matt suffers a heart attack and later dies. Father Callahan's faith is not strong enough to fight off Barlow, and he goes crazy and leaves town. Barlow destroys Straker to punish him for letting Mark escape.

While the two groups make contact as one tries to destroy the other, they operate in different time frames. The night belongs to the vampires, and the day to the hunters. The vampire hunters are always racing against the clock because they must discover Barlow's hiding place during the day, when he is powerless. The vampires spend the night attacking new victims. Fewer and fewer people move about the town during the day. Parkins Gillespie, the police chief, knows what's happening, but he decides to leave town. Jimmy dies when he falls into a trap set by Barlow. Mark and Ben go after Barlow. They finally open his coffin just as the sun sets. Ben manages to destroy Barlow, and he and Mark escape just as the vampires come to life. The heroes have not destroyed all the vampires by the time the main section of the novel ends. The epilogue picks up where the prologue left off. We finally begin to understand the puzzles of the prologue. We now know who the man and the boy are, and we realize that they have come back to finish the job of killing the vampires in 'salem's Lot.

The epilogue opens with a series of newspaper clippings from Ben's scrapbook. The dates range from November 19, 1975, to June 4, 1976. The reader may remember that the main text opened on September 5, 1975. The reader also now understands how to look at the information. The names are not important, but the series of events described means that 'salem's Lot is not dead. People still disappear; some hear strange noises; police suspect a wild dog pack. Each article ends in an unfinished sentence, suggesting uncompleted business.

The next section of the epilogue begins with another, less specific date. "The tall man and the boy arrived in Portland in mid-September and stayed at a local motel for three weeks" (423). We have no trouble identifying the tall man and the boy this time, even though King repeats the narrative style of the prologue. But although the characters are not identified, everything else becomes more and more exact. We learn of other events occurring in 'salem's Lot, and King gives the exact date the man decides to act, October 6. We still have no idea how they plan to deal with the remaining vampires.

The characters are finally given names now that the connections among prologue, epilogue, and novel are clear. We learn about the high fire index in Maine, almost as high as the year of the big fire. We suddenly understand why Ben has been waiting. Ben relives memories of the town. He discusses their options with the boy. A fire will destroy many vampires and force them out of their hiding places. "A couple of people just looking in obvious places could do well. Maybe it could be finished in 'salem's Lot by the time the first snow flew. Maybe it would never be finished" (427). Ben also believes in the purifying power of fire. He deliberately drops his cigarette in a pile of leaves in the spot where someone years ago also got careless with a cigarette. The novel ends as Mark and Ben drive off; the fire begins to burn, fanned by the wind from the west.

## CHARACTERS

We have seen how King introduces characters. We learn about them in bits and pieces. At times it is hard to tell who is going to be important to the story. Many of the chapter titles are the names of characters. The several chapters dealing with Ben or Susan carry their names. But sometimes a chapter title is not a good clue about the importance of a character. "Danny Glick and Others" (74) opens after the disappearance of Ralph, Danny's brother, and ends with Danny's death. We never really learn much about Danny. Some of the more important characters, such as Barlow or Jimmy, have no chapters named after them. King organizes *'Salem's Lot* so that we watch the good characters operate and learn about them. We seldom see the evil characters and know almost nothing about them.

### Ben and Mark

Once we identify the boy and the man from the prologue, we know that they are important characters. King presents these characters through their actions. We first see Ben as the man who is good both with his hands and his mind; he fixes cars and writes a novel. Mark is the boy who doesn't want to read the newspaper and who joins the church. The first time we learn Mark's name he is the new boy who outsmarts the school bully. Their actions establish them as characters who will be brave and smart enough to deal with Barlow. Mark is also associated with the models Ralph and Danny want to see. Mark knows about horror. He believes in the power of Dracula, Frankenstein, the mummy, and the wolfman. His belief and his knowledge save him from becoming a vampire.

Ben, the adult, grows as the novel progresses. He has to come to terms with his past in order to survive. He accepts the reality of what he encountered in the Marsten House as a child. That acceptance also leads him to believe in the reality of the vampires. He begins to understand the difference between the things he can change in the present and the things he must live with in the past. He faces the death of two women he loves, Miranda and Susan. By the end of the novel he sees that he must go beyond love of the individual. Just saving Mark is not enough for him. He must also return and save those who might be attacked by the vampires. Ben is the character who provides the connection for all of the people in 'salem's Lot. He is also the first of King's author/heroes. King suggests that writers' belief in an imaginary world helps them survive when they must deal with the supernatural.

## The Vampire Hunters

The rest of the vampire hunters, introduced at various points in the novel, are somewhat developed as individuals. These characters most often perform functions relating to the development of the plot. Susan is the most completely presented of these secondary characters. We see her in relation to Ben and interacting with her family. Susan is representative of King's early female characters because she often falls into stereotypical roles. When she first meets Ben she is a young, naive artist who wants to go to the big city but doesn't know how. She reacts with predictable negativity with her mother, who would like her to settle down with Floyd. We feel that she is attracted to Ben in part because she knows her mother won't approve. Susan dies when she investigates the Marsten House without the men and is caught by Straker to fulfill the traditional function of bride of the vampire.

Matt is a typical high school English teacher. He runs the drama club and drinks too much in the local bar. His connection to young people helps him believe in vampires, but this belief also destroys him. His body betrays him with heart failure because he does not have the courage to face his fears. He does not have the "heart" to act when he hears Mike being attacked. He has the mind to connect all of the events and research their basis in folklore and myth. He can explain what is happening to the others, but he is not strong enough to follow them into action. Jimmy Cody, however, is a man of action, a doctor willing to look beyond science for the answers to questions raised by the strange deaths of his patients. Jimmy goes with Mark to destroy vampires because he would be known to the living members of 'salem's Lot, while Ben is a stranger. He is smart enough to figure out where Barlow hides, but he moves too quickly and falls into the vampire's trap. Jimmy is defined only by his actions.

Father Callahan also represents a stereotype, the drunken priest. He longs for bigger challenges than he has found in 'salem's Lot, but he is too far gone when he finally gets a chance to take a stand. Susan's death and the failure of his religion are two of the major surprises King gives us. We expect a priest to be important in fighting the vampire. Callahan's faith fails him; the cross loses its power because he does not have enough faith to face Barlow without it. King connects the loss of faith with the loss of soul. After Callahan's cross loses its power he must drink the vampire's blood. But he becomes a wanderer, waiting for his new master to claim him. Once he has truly lost his faith he has no place in the world. While we sympathize with him, we see his failure as a flaw in his character. If the other characters are defined by the actions they take, Callahan is defined by the action Barlow forces on him.

## THEME

King explores three themes in *'Salem's Lot*: the traditional battle between good and evil, the effect of maturity on the imagination, and the failure of the traditional family. He uses a traditional literary form, the vampire novel, to explore modern themes that concern us in our own lives. While we can examine these themes separately, they are connected in the novel because they are all part of the concept of the confusion of boundaries in modern life. King explores how we are being forced to abandon traditional distinctions while at the same time we set up new, artificial divisions in our lives. We have difficulty seeing the difference between good and evil. We break the continuity between child and adult by creating false separations between these stages in our lives. We have also allowed the traditional organization of the family to disintegrate without finding a good substitute.

In *'Salem's Lot* King adopts the conflict between good and evil from the vampire tradition. Unlike ghosts or other monsters of horror, vampires can easily create new vampires. The evil they represent spreads like a disease, posing a serious threat to society because they can quickly transform humans into creatures who can contaminate others. *'Salem's Lot* is the first King novel to be concerned with the spread of evil; he examines other variations of this problem in such later works as *The Stand* and *The Tommyknockers*. In these works King is concerned with evil which attacks the structure of society. Once the vampires take over the town, 'salem's Lot ceases to exist. The police cannot operate, businesses fail, families are destroyed. The traditional connections between people are broken. While vampires destroy the structures which keep society operating, they also reverse natural laws. The dead come back to life. Vampires form new families of unrelated victims and operate at night when humans sleep. The town is dead during the day, but it comes awake at night with the vampires. The existence of those who live during the day and those who become undead at night blurs the differences between life and death.

Unlike ghosts or monsters, vampires pose a threat too strong for one person to overcome. People must band together to deal with an evil which threatens to destroy society. Characters with traditional expertise in the areas of general knowledge, science, and religion usually work together to destroy the evil. In *'Salem's Lot* Matt, Jimmy, and Father Callahan are not successful. Matt's scholarship adds to the understanding of the vampire, as do Jimmy's medicine and Callahan's religion. But these men ultimately fail because they do not work together. When they separate Barlow can successfully attack them and destroy them. Ben and Mark are successful because they form a new family unit.

King shows that new kinds of heroes are necessary to fight modern evil. While knowledge, science, and religion are important in modern life, we suffer from a lack of imagination and creativity. These are the two qualities Mark and Ben bring to the fight. Mark has the imaginative qualities present in children, and Ben has the ability both to retain these powers as an adult and to transform them into art. In King's world imagination and creativity give people the power to understand evil and defeat it. Callahan fails because his belief fails him. Ben succeeds because he can believe in evil the way children believe, without question. Ben and Mark can ignore the border between the real world and the world of the imagination. In the modern world we no longer have the imagination to believe in what we cannot actually see. King fears that this loss makes us easy victims of evil.

King is concerned about what happens to people when they forget their youth. Children are important characters in many of his novels because they still live in a world where anything is possible. Adults need their connections to the world of childhood to survive, and children cannot conquer evil alone. The group of children in *It* must return to Derry as adults to really destroy the monster. Mark trusts Ben because this adult has not lost the ability to believe in the world of childhood. Writers must believe in the new worlds they create for these worlds to come alive for the reader. King sees this creativity as an extension into the adult world of a child's powers to create play worlds. We cannot really see good or evil. We can only see the effects of good and evil actions. We can believe in good and evil, but we are limited by our reliance on science and rational thought. For us, vampires exist only in books and films. Mark's and Ben's ability to believe in evil that crosses the boundary from fiction to reality allows them to destroy it.

While the group is important in dealing with evil, King would still like to locate power for good within the traditional family at this point in his career. We join King in wanting Susan, Ben, and Mark to form a new family. But they do not succeed. Instead, the novel is full of unsuccessful families with abusive mothers, distant fathers, and disobedient children. King explores the relationship between family members and outsiders as the crossing of boundaries. We think of borders as separating one country from another, or of family structures as separating insiders and outsiders or dividing adults from children. King shows that none of these borders is solid. At the beginning of the novel Ben and Mark cross the border from one country to another. For King the modern family is no longer a strong unit which can unite to fight the evil that attacks it. Too often, as we see in *'Salem's Lot*, the evil comes from within the family unit as family members become vampires. Adults fail to believe in the threat of vampires because they have crossed a border, leaving the child's imagination behind.

Modern problems do not cause the evil in *'Salem's Lot*. Vampires do not succeed because we have developed such confidence in the world of science that we deny the possibility of their existence. People's distance from their childhood imaginations and their lack of connection and trust allow the evil to spread. The horror in this novel comes from outside our world. King believes that evil attracts evil. The Marsten House draws Straker and Barlow to it. But once the evil enters the community it becomes a part of it. The vampire comes from outside of the community, but his bite introduces his poison into 'salem's Lot. Ben wants to know how long it takes to become part of the community. The sheriff tells him people could live in the Lot for twenty years before being accepted. Yet Barlow creates a new family in days.

The way to defeat evil is to form new units without strict boundaries, like the group that joins together to fight the vampire or the kind of family Ben and Mark create. These groups are constructed out of need and trust and love, not the artificial bonds of blood relationships and town traditions. The vampires build new families with blood ties, setting up the same old boundaries. King also challenges the division between adult and child. In order to survive one has to be either an adult who has the imagination of a child or a child who has the maturity to act like an adult.

King suggests that modern evil may not be totally destroyed. The novel ends with Ben setting a fire. We do not see the results. We do not know how successful Ben and Mark will be in destroying all of the vampires. At the end of a horror novel we traditionally expect evil to be conquered by good. King's refusal to show the defeat of evil is the final blurring of boundaries in *'Salem's Lot*. Modern life is too uncertain for King to give us the absolute certainty that good will destroy evil.

## ALTERNATE READING: THE DEVELOPING GENRE—*DRACULA* AND *'SALEM'S LOT*

King is generally associated with the horror genre. Readers who choose his novels expect to read about frightening events. We also expect these events to have a source in the supernatural. If we think we are going to read a novel about vampires, we may believe in a set of rules that vampires must follow. We know that vampires can't stand sunlight, that most are afraid of crosses and holy water, and that they sleep in coffins, usually on some of their native soil. Vampires can change people into new vampires, although the rules for how this happens can vary. All of these rules about imaginary creatures are a way of defining one part of the horror genre.

Bram Stoker's *Dracula* established most of the rules for vampires. In *Danse Macabre* (38–39) King presents his view of the relationship between *'Salem's Lot* and *Dracula*. He uses the image of a racquetball game with *'Salem's Lot* as the racquet and *Dracula* as the wall to describe his creative process. King lists the staking of Susan (Lucy Westenra is the corresponding character in *Dracula*) and the drinking of the vampire's blood by Father Callahan (Mina Harker in *Dracula*) in his novel as scenes parallel to those in Stoker's. If we compare the two books we can see the influence of the older book on the newer one. We can also see how the genre and its rules operate differently with the passage of time.

King uses elements of *Dracula* to develop the idea of vampires in his novel. *Dracula*, briefly, is the story of the Count's invasion of Victorian England and his attempt to establish a new home and a new group of vampires. In addition to the idea of infecting an area with the disease of vampirism, *'Salem's Lot* also shares aspects of *Dracula*'s style. Stoker's novel is written entirely in journal entries, articles, and letters. King briefly uses many of these devices in his book. But there are also important differences between the two books. Barlow is not as sexually interesting as Dracula. While Dracula forces Mina to drink his blood to make her his bride, Barlow shows his power to destroy a man of God by forcing Father Callahan to commit the same act.

Both novels open with journeys. In *Dracula*, Jonathan Harker goes from west to east. Ben and Mark go from east to west and turn around. They try to run away from what has happened but realize that they can't. Jonathan travels to meet the vampire, to bring knowledge to Count Dracula. He has done his research and is prepared to act as an agent for the Count. As readers, we may be slightly more wary; we may think he is overconfident. The man and the boy already know all there is to know about their journey. They travel to bring an end to events that have already happened. But the reader has only a vague idea of their goals. And the reader moves from their decision to return to yet another journey in the first chapter of the main body of the novel. While Ben's first return to 'salem's Lot is, on the surface, like that of Jonathan, the reader cannot approach it in the same way. The events King presents in the prologue, especially the newspaper reports, have already made us aware that something awful has happened. Unlike Harker, Ben does not travel for business, and he is not discovering new territory. Like the unnamed protagonists of the prologue, Ben returns to 'salem's Lot to confront an episode from his past. Both Harker and Ben share similar destinations, strange, evil buildings which dominate the landscape. The Marsten House is newer than Castle Dracula, but it, too, has a history. Ben already has a connection with the house. He does not come to Jerusalem's Lot to explain the rental of another house. He wants to rent the Marsten House as a way of gaining control over his nightmares. Unlike Jonathan's connection to Dracula, Ben has no business with Barlow or Straker. At the points of seemingly greatest similarity between the two novels important differences emerge.

As with most vampire literature, the aim of the central characters is to destroy the vampire and eliminate the plague this figure has created. King can take a long time introducing his vampire, because once such a figure is operating our familiarity with the genre helps us understand what is happening. The endings of both novels reverse the actions that opened them. Ben goes back to 'salem's Lot and Jonathan follows Dracula back to Transylvania. Events begin to happen quickly once the characters realize that they are safe only during the day. Each novel creates suspense when characters race to destroy vampires before nightfall. They are constantly looking to see where the sun is and how late it is getting. As they race to destroy the vampire or vampires, central characters sacrifice themselves for the success of the group. The main text of *Dracula* ends with the death of Quincey Morris, one of the band who chased and helped destroy Dracula. At the end of *'Salem's Lot* Ben returns briefly to the town before heading west. He buries Jimmy, who also died trying to destroy a vampire.

Both novels have epilogues which deal with events after the main action. *Dracula* ends on a more hopeful note than King's novel. Dracula's destruction has meant the end of the threat of the vampire. Jonathan can make a family holiday out of a visit to Transylvania and the ruins of Castle Dracula. Seven years have passed, and no trace remains of the events. For the reader this is just one example of the difficulty of proving the reality of the story. The horror genre relies on our belief that such things could possibly happen. The novel explains why we won't be able to see the castle if we visit the site. Jonathan also explains that no documents exist which could demonstrate proof of the events. We either accept or reject the story based on our ability to accept the possibilities suggested by the genre. Jonathan and the others do not care. "We want no proofs; we ask none to believe us!" He only cares that his son understand the truth. "Already he knows her sweetness and loving care; later he will understand how some men so loved her, that they did dare much for her sake" (332). The novel ends by maintaining the importance of the family and heterosexual relationships.

*'Salem's Lot* does not end with the triumph of the group working together to rid the world of a single, final menace. Like Jonathan, Ben retraces his steps, but he does it for a different kind of ending. He burns the manuscript he has been writing, a story of the Marsten House. He also destroys his last connection with the house and its roots in his childhood, the glass snow globe he grabbed the first time he visited the house. He now sees it as an evil object and imagines the vampire's face looking out at him from the gingerbread house. But the face is his own. When he throws it in the corner it breaks. "He left without waiting to see what might leak out of it" (418). Ben leaves 'salem's Lot and its welcome sign to return to the motel and Mark. "He began to drive south toward Mark, toward his life" (419). But as the reader knows, the story does not end with this trip out of 'salem's Lot, because this ending is obviously the

beginning of the prologue of the novel. The circular action of *'Salem's Lot* takes the characters back to their past. It makes the reader understand how hard it is to escape the powerful evil of the vampire.

Unlike *Dracula, 'Salem's Lot* closes with only a hope that the vampire plague is ended. Even the fire is just beginning. Society survives in the nontraditional family of Ben and Mark. In this uncertain world some things do remain. Mark has a vial of holy water. The religion whose priest fails in his confrontation with evil is revived in the belief of the boy, Mark. The artist also survives; we know that Ben has already written another novel since he and Mark left 'salem's Lot. The vampires seem to have been contained in and around the town. The newspaper reports tell only of the incidents in the vicinity of 'salem's Lot.

While the two novels may explore different values with their central characters, and while different values may be sustained in each ending, they do share a certain core. The open ending of *'Salem's Lot* is not really disturbing. In a sense no trace of this novel remains, because we will not find the town on any map. Evil remains active on an individual level, and people still have the power to confront it and possibly control it. They survive and eventually resume their lives. The emphasis may be different, but each novel in its own way upholds a view of the world where traditional values remain. King believes that this return to order is one of the values of the genre. The reader can experience evil without fearing its effect.

A comparison of the two novels shows how King develops his own version of the horror novel. He builds on the traditions established by authors like Stoker and adapts them to the modern world. Father Callahan's failure of faith, which makes his cross useless, would not happen in *Dracula.* Each novel mirrors the beliefs of its time. Stoker's evil comes from a royal stranger who threatens ordinary people and sometimes carefully selects his victims. For King the real evil comes from our family and friends, who can suddenly turn on us. Count Dracula infects only a few people. The ideals of family and friendship are protected. King tells us that the strange things we see happening around us may have a supernatural source. We have to be careful who we believe and trust. A comparison of the two shows both the changes in beliefs and the differences in the ways an author presents these changes.

4

# *The Shining*
## (1977)

*The Shining*, Stephen King's third novel, explores another aspect of the horror genre, the ghost story. Genre generally refers to the categories used by both author and reader to classify a work. We select the horror genre because we have certain expectations about how the fiction will be presented (see Chapter 2). In the ghost story the origin of the horror comes from evil spirits who usually haunt a specific location. We expect these spirits to become visible to some of the characters and to influence their actions. Ghost stories are often set in remote, old mansions where the characters begin to sense that they are not really alone. Former occupants interact with the current residents. While ghosts can be good or bad, those in *The Shining* are evil. King isolates his central characters in a resort hotel in Colorado which is closed for the winter. Gradually the hotel comes alive with the ghosts of the past, who have turned it into an evil place. Jack Torrance, a teacher who lost his job because he beat up a student, brings his family to the Overlook Hotel. From the beginning we know there are going to be problems in this family. Jack, a reformed alcoholic, gets a job as winter caretaker through the influence of a friend. Mr. Ullman, the manager, is uneasy about letting a family stay in the hotel because the roads are closed from late October to April. A former caretaker, Delbert Grady, also an alcoholic, went crazy, killed his wife and children, and then committed suicide there. Jack thinks himself immune to such problems and moves his family into the hotel.

An introductory note to *The Shining* states that the Overlook Hotel is a creation of the author's imagination, but King and his wife did stay at the Stanley Hotel in Colorado just as it was closing for the season and spent one night in room 217. They paid their bill with an American Express card, the only one for which the hotel still had charge slips. Stephen was even served a drink by a bartender named Grady. The idea for the book came to him during this brief stay (Beahm, *Stephen King Story* 69). This book was King's first hardcover best seller.

The Colorado location is one of King's rare explorations of territory outside of Maine. He opens the novel with an excerpt from Edgar Allan Poe's epigraph "The Masque of the Red Death." In this story the wealthy guests of a prince have shut themselves up in a castle hoping to escape the plague of the red death, which is killing people in the countryside. The excerpt King chooses deals with the party at the end of the story. The clock chimes, indicating the approach of death, but the dance continues. The party resembles those that take place at the Overlook in the novel. But in *The Shining* all the partygoers are already dead; they come back to life as ghosts. In *Danse Macabre* he discusses his interest in how the haunted house operates in the genre, an idea he had already explored in *'Salem's Lot*. "*The Shining* is set in the apotheosis of the Bad Place: not a haunted house, but a haunted hotel, with a different 'real' horror movie playing in almost every one of its guest rooms and suites" (254). King places a family which is already in crisis in this evil setting. People and place interact to create horror which is both natural and supernatural.

## PLOT DEVELOPMENT

The original version of *The Shining* had a prologue ("Before the Play") and an epilogue ("After the Play"), the pattern used in *'Salem's Lot* (Beahm, *Stephen King Story* 77). The final version opens with Jack's job interview at the Overlook. This section, called "Prefatory Matters," is followed by four more large sections: "Closing Day," "The Wasp's Nest," "Snowbound," and "Matters of Life and Death." These divisions are comparable to the five acts of a play, connecting the structure of the novel to the play the central character is writing. The sections are further divided into chapters. The final chapter title, "Epilogue/Summer," keeps something of King's original plan. While these titles are functional and descriptive, they divide the novel into longer and longer sections. The first two sections introduce the characters and the hotel and cover a day each. But they refer back to events in the lives of the characters and the hotel over a long period of time. The next two sections deal with events over several days, and the connections between them are complex. In both, characters begin to have encounters with the hotel's past. The end of "The Wasp's Nest" overlaps in time with the opening of the next section: Danny's exploration of room 217. The final section continues this overlapping pattern to give a sense of a world gone crazy. The last chapter takes us forward to the next year and lets us know a little about the characters before we leave them.

King gives a great deal of information in the opening chapters. He quickly gives insights into the central characters as well as clues which alert us to future problems. We expect the novel to deal with horror, and we look for points which will take us into the genre. King moves immediately into the minds of the characters and lets us read their thoughts. The conflicting views he presents of Jack leave us wondering what to think of this man. We hear the same things he does about the hotel and follow his reactions. We tend to agree with him that the hotel's past history should not prevent the manager from giving him the job. We know that the previous caretaker killed himself and his wife and children, but this first horror seems to be part of the natural rather than the supernatural world. We also meet Mr. Ullman, who is concerned only about running the hotel and making money.

We move from Jack's mind to that of his wife, Wendy (short for Winnifred). We meet Wendy and their son, Danny, as they wait for Jack to return from the interview. As Wendy reflects on their life, we learn that Jack was a teacher at a private secondary school until he was fired for attacking a student. The next chapter connects two kinds of violence and foreshadows the climax of the novel. While Jack is learning how to maintain the boiler, he recalls discovering that his three-year-old son had poured beer on the manuscript of his play. Jack's reaction shocks us: he twists and breaks Danny's arm. The story of his explosion is quickly followed by an explanation of the pressure in the boiler. The pressure creeps, and if Jack doesn't regulate it twice a day, the hotel can explode. The old boiler can't take much pressure. We immediately make the connection between the two kinds of pressure and the two explosions. We also learn about another hotel guest who couldn't stand the pressure, a woman whose young lover left her. The maid found her dead in the bathtub, an ugly suicide. As the chapter ends, Jack, who is on the wagon, is wishing for a drink.

The opening of the next chapter suggests the relationship between

Danny and Jack. Danny, who has been waiting for Jack to return from the interview, drinks his milk. The father is thirsty, and the son drinks. King uses various devices in this chapter to place us in the mind of a five-year-old child. But sometimes Danny's language seems too adult. We gradually learn of Danny's special ability. He can read minds and see things hidden from most people. The part of his mind identified with this power takes the form of an imaginary playmate named Tony who shows him things or leads him to information. His playmate helps Danny locate the trunk which holds Jack's play. The movers had placed it out of sight under the stairs. With this evidence of Tony's powers we become concerned when the playmate shows Danny a series of images, including a jar of wasps and a snowstorm. Danny also sees a building with part of a new roof—an image of the Overlook in the future after Jack repairs the roof. Danny also sees a key word which will be repeated many times in the novel: "REDRUM." Tony's final image is a horrible shape swinging a mallet and chasing Danny.

In these opening chapters King outlines the significant events of the novel. The meaning of these images is unclear, but they serve two key functions in *The Shining*. From the beginning we know that terrible things are going to happen to the Torrances at the hotel. There are too many indications of violence past and future. These repeated images function like memories. By the end of the novel we recognize these events as they happen. The ghosts in the hotel make the past come alive and affect the present and the future. Jack can't escape these images and is finally controlled by them. Our path through the book is also controlled by these images, and they become part of our memory as well. We cannot escape as long as we continue to read. We, too, come under the influence of the past and its ghosts.

King's early novels are structured to pull the characters along. If they make the wrong decision at the beginning, there is no escape for them. Jack, already trapped by his past, must take this job. It is his last hope. If the hotel draws him in, he is a partner because his circumstances give him no room to move. King places his characters in situations filled with pressure, and we watch to see if they can survive. We are also pulled along by the narrative. King organizes the book to catch us in another way, gradually making us believe in the possibility of the supernatural. He leads us across the line from the real to the unreal without our realizing where we are. He even gives us a chance to escape, but we are in the middle of the horror before we realize it.

King first has us believe in Danny. We know Danny is a good boy who would not lie. We may think he has an overactive imagination when he sees Tony and the images. But then we meet Dick Hallorann, the African American cook at the Overlook. Hallorann tells Danny that he shines harder than anyone the cook has ever met (80). Hallorann realizes that Danny doesn't know that other people share his gift. We might not believe in the kind of shining the cook describes, where people can talk without words. But we all recognize people who have had some kind of ability to read others' thoughts. Hallorann explains that most of these people are not even aware of their powers. We just think they are thoughtful when they know how we feel. By reducing the shining to simple insights we may have experienced, King leads us slowly to a position where we may believe in the possibility of Danny's powers.

King uses the same technique to get us to believe in the power of the ghosts in the hotel. Jack finds a wasps' nest, uses a bug bomb to kill the wasps, and gives the nest to Danny. Later that night the wasps come alive and sting Danny. We see a logical explanation. The wasps weren't really dead the first time. Jack next encounters strange events when he is trimming the topiary animals. The hotel has a series of hedge animals, including a rabbit, a dog, a horse, a cow, and three lions. He clips the rabbit and then goes to look at the playground. When he turns back to the animals they have moved. They come toward him, and he manages to go around them and get back to the hotel. We can think that he is just imagining things, that his mind is playing tricks on him. But we may also believe just a little, enough so that we are ready to accept their attacking Danny and Hallorann at the end of the novel.

By the end of the third part of the novel snow blocks the roads to the hotel. The hotel also begins to isolate the characters. The ghosts begin to take over Jack's mind. He acts without realizing what he has done. The hotel tries to get Danny too. Unable to resist the call of room 217, he takes the key and enters the room. On page 217 of the novel Danny finds the dead body, the ghost of the suicide, which haunts this room. The section ends as Danny tries to open the door, which now seems to be locked, to escape this horrible ghost. In the next section, "Snowbound," the ghost chases Danny while his mother and father nap. Jack thinks about his relationship with his father while he dreams. His thoughts move from his love of his father to the moment when his father attacks his mother and sends her to the hospital. King directly connects this information to Danny by leaving him in trouble while Jack dreams of another father/son relationship.

Time moves quickly in this section. Wendy wakens and looks for

Danny. Her fear that Jack may have hurt him seems to be confirmed when they see bruises on Danny's neck. The misunderstandings between husband and wife become critical. Wendy wants to take Danny off the mountain to the doctor. Jack acts without thinking, controlled by the ghosts. He smashes the radio and disables the snowmobile. One day, while playing in the snow, Danny is pursued by the hedge creatures. The incidents increase until the end of the chapter, when Danny has a vision of Jack chasing him with a mallet. Danny sends out a telepathic call for help to Hallorann.

Section five, "Matters of Life and Death," opens as Hallorann, who finally receives Danny's call, makes his way back to the hotel in a blizzard. King often substitutes another male like Hallorann for a defective father when children are in trouble. While one father fails Danny, another comes to rescue him. Wendy manages to lock up Jack in the pantry, but Danny realizes that the hotel is coming alive. Grady, the ghost, releases Jack after he promises to give Danny to the hotel. Jack knows he will have to kill Wendy to get Danny. Jack pushes open the door and finds that Grady has left him both alcohol and a murder weapon, a roque mallet. The tension in the novel increases with the danger. While Wendy and Danny are threatened by Jack, Hallorann has to face both real and ghostly attacks. As he reaches the hotel, the hedge animals attack. While Hallorann deals with them, Wendy, even though Jack has injured her back, manages to escape after Jack traps her in the bathroom. Jack then knocks out Hallorann. Another kind of help returns. Tony, who has not been able to get through to Danny, appears briefly and tells him that he will be able to remember what his father has forgotten. While Jack looks for Danny, Wendy finds Hallorann.

The final confrontation between father and son ends when Danny tells his father that the hotel has taken over Jack. Danny knows that Jack has been seduced by the lies he has been told. The remnant that remains of the real Jack tells Danny to run. Danny kisses his father's hand before he leaves, and suddenly remembers what his father forgot: the steam has not been released from the boiler. It is going to explode. Hallorann, Wendy, and Danny escape as the hotel erupts. When Hallorann looks back he sees a strange shape, like a swarm of hornets, emerge in the flames. They are met by rescuers coming up the mountain. The hotel is destroyed.

The epilogue shows the result of these events. The survivors are damaged, but they have resumed their lives. They meet in Florida at the lodge where Hallorann works. Nine months have passed, but Wendy still wears a back brace. Danny still has dreams, but they are becoming less frequent. Hallorann and Danny talk. Hallorann explains the world to Danny as if he were his father. Danny has had experiences which no six-year-old child should have undergone. Hallorann cannot explain why evil occurs. He counsels Danny to accept what has happened, grieve for his father, and get on with his life. While the scars remain, these characters can now look toward the future.

## CHARACTERS

King concentrates on the family unit in *The Shining*. He admits to exploring his own feelings about being a father in the character of Jack Torrance. He also wanted to deal with the dark side of being a parent, the bad parent (Beahm, *Stephen King Story* 70). While he is most concerned with the father/son relationship, King also deals with problem marriages and the effect isolation can have on them. Except for the hotel staff members introduced early in the novel, the only other important characters are Dick Hallorann, the Overlook, and its ghosts. The rest of the people who influence the action appear as memories. Their actions occur before the novel begins. Jack's friend, Albert Shockley, is both benefactor and drinking buddy. Jack has two phone conversations with him during the novel. George Hatfield, whom Jack drops from the school debating team, retaliates by slashing Jack's tires. Jack responds by severely beating him. The four most important characters, Jack, Wendy, Danny, and Hallorann, have chapters in which they present their point of view.

### Jack

Jack and Danny are the major characters in *The Shining*. King concentrates on them as individuals and on their relationship as father and son. Jack's actions and reactions characterize him. The first time we see him we are not sure whether we should like him. In the horror genre we expect to identify with the central character. Even if we do not like someone in the beginning, brave actions later in the novel may redeem the character. Since we meet Jack first and he is the male adult in the story, we expect him to be the hero. But King immediately suggests that we should be wary of Jack. We learn about Delbert Grady, who shares many of Jack's traits. King shows us Jack's violent temper twice with his reactions to Danny and George. While we may not like Ullman, we also don't like the superior attitude Jack takes toward him.

Our view of Jack changes slightly when we see him from Danny's perspective. Danny still loves his father even after his arm is broken. We also learn that Danny feared the word "DIVORCE" after his injury. Although he wants his parents to stay together, he does have certain fears about his father. He is afraid his father will do the "Bad Thing." We soon figure out that the Bad Thing is drinking and the violence that can result from it. We move from Danny's thoughts of his father's violence to further evidence of Jack's character. As he calls Al Shockley to thank him for the job, he recalls their relationship, which resembles that of many drinking buddies. They met at Stovington Preparatory Academy, where Jack taught and Al was a member of the board of directors and a tennis coach. Jack recalls their final night of drinking together. Jack's marriage is almost over; Al is already separated from his wife. They are both very drunk as Al drives home. They crash into a bike in the middle of the road, certain they've killed its rider. They are lucky; there is no child. Al immediately decides to stop drinking, but Jack almost commits suicide. While this further evidence of Jack's lack of stability certainly worries us, we admire his ability to reform. He stops drinking and does not begin again even during the incident which costs him his job. We sympathize with him about this event. We would all have violent thoughts if we caught someone slashing our tires. We may even begin to feel a kind of identification with Jack over this episode. King moves us into a closer relationship with this character by revealing the negative first and then showing his more positive traits. Our realization that .we may share some attitudes with Jack draws us into his world.

King continues to reinforce the positive side of Jack's character. He wants us to relax about Jack for a while. Because we get closer to him and understand him, Jack's final disintegration is more frightening. King also continues to suggest that we should not get too close to Jack. Jack's first major crisis as caretaker comes when he discovers a wasps' nest while repairing the roof. We are relieved that Jack seems to be working so well, even though the chapter opens with his violent reaction when he gets stung by a wasp. But we know we might react the same way. We follow Jack's thoughts as he replays the recent events in his life. We also begin to understand the cause of much of Jack's behavior, his childhood at the hands of an abusive father. We are worried when Jack experiences everything as a victim rather than admitting responsibility for his actions. We like Jack's relationship with Danny and are happy to learn that he is working on his play. We may even remember that he has been working on it for a long time. Many of the incidents that define his character involve the play. We are sorry when the wasps' nest comes alive and the wasps sting Danny. This episode seems to confirm Jack's view that things happen to him.

Gradually we understand that Jack's inability to take responsibility for his actions is exactly what makes it possible for the hotel to take him over. If he cannot make his own decisions or refuses to see alternatives, the hotel can control him. Wendy finally convinces him to leave the Overlook, but he cannot see a way out of his dilemma. If they leave, they have no place to go, no money, no hope. The hotel wins. He suddenly realizes that the hotel really wants Danny and believes in the events he has denied. He recognizes the power he shares with Danny; he knows the hedges did move. But the same voice which tells him these truths goes on to suggest another truth. The minute they hit a town he will go back to the bar. When he finally acts, he is controlled by a false voice, which has come from the hotel and which begins to possess him.

### Danny

King traces Jack's background and the love/hate relationship with his father which makes him vulnerable to the influence of the Overlook. Danny's love/hate relationship with Jack extends this pattern to the next generation. But Danny is saved because his powers help him unite the various elements of his personality. The shine gives him the ability to see beyond his love for his father into the negative sides of the man's character. He also has Tony both as a source of information and as a way to keep some of his conflicts outside of his own mind. When he sees Tony he knows this friend is really part of him and his father. Tony shares his name with Danny's grandfather (Mark Anthony Torrance), Jack (John Anthony Torrance), and Danny (Daniel Anthony Torrance). When Danny looks closely at Tony it is like looking in a magic mirror. Danny sees Tony as his future, "a halfling caught between father and son, a ghost of both, a fusion" (420).

Danny is the positive reflection of Jack, good where his father is evil. But image and reflection are connected. At the end of the novel, Danny is able to break the connection because his father is no longer recognizable. He finally understands that he has not been seeing his father as he really is. His view of his father changes when all of the images Tony has shown him come true. He finally understands that REDRUM is the mirror image of MURDER. Danny is also able to break with Jack because he can call on Dick Hallorann, his other "father." The connection between these two characters goes beyond their sharing the shine. Danny's nickname, "Doc," is close to "Dick." When Hallorann immediately knows Danny's nickname we have evidence of Hallorann's power and the connection between them.

### Hallorann

Hallorann's character is not as carefully developed as that of Jack or Danny. But we do spend some time with him when he struggles through a snowstorm to rescue the boy. Hallorann's function as the good father who takes over when the blood relative fails is common in early King novels. One of the terrors of childhood is the realization that our parents can't always protect us. While King may take these fears further by giving Danny an evil father, he balances this by giving him Hallorann. Hallorann also functions as the person who explains the supernatural. At some point in the horror story, we need to understand how the supernatural operates and how it relates to our idea of the natural world. Hallorann gives Danny the understanding which will help him survive. Danny, as any child might, disobeys Hallorann when he goes to room 217, which Hallorann has told him to avoid. But Hallorann is the good father who understands rather than punishes the mistakes of childhood. His connection to both Danny and Jack is further emphasized by the hedge animals' attack on all three of them. Jack assaults Hallorann but cannot kill him. Hallorann is the one who helps Wendy and Danny escape from the hotel. But even the good father is tempted. When Hallorann enters the shed to get blankets, he is attracted to a mallet from the same set as the one Jack has used to attack the family. Hallorann is able to resist, but King does not really explain why this character can avoid the voices of the Overlook.

### Wendy

Wendy is also not as fully developed as Danny and Jack. We learn little about her beyond her difficult relationship with her mother. This conflict is meant to serve as a balance with Jack's relationship with his father. But Wendy has no special powers. She doesn't interest the hotel and seldom experiences its force. She can see only the results of the supernatural events in the novel. She can make connections between the natural and the supernatural. She links the possibility that Danny may have special powers to a circumstance surrounding his birth. He was born with a piece of skin over his face, known as a caul, a phenomenon traditionally associated with the ability to see the future. She cannot share Jack's or Danny's experiences with supernatural forces. She tries to save her son, but she cannot overcome Jack's power. Too often her only role is to remain his victim.

### Overlook Hotel

The Overlook Hotel becomes the real source of much of the action in the novel. The evil forces come alive when they are exposed to Jack's personality and Danny's powers. The hotel is the "bad place," an echo of Jack's drinking, which Danny calls the "Bad Thing." King does not locate the evil in the hotel in one room or associate it with one person or event. Instead, he suggests that capitalism, the constant need to make money from the hotel, serves as a magnet for the evil the place attracts. Money brings the gangsters to the hotel and causes the gang war in which they are killed. A woman commits suicide because she learns she can't buy love. Grady is forced to isolate himself and his family because, like Jack, he needs money. Jack falls fully under the influence of the hotel when he finds a scrapbook among some old receipts that details its history. The hotel destroys itself at the end because of money. It becomes a symbol of the abuse of power which can come with money.

## THEME

In *The Shining* King uses ghosts, fairy tales, children's literature, and classics of the horror tradition to explore two related themes: the negative elements in parent/child relationships and how evil attacks childhood innocence. He explores how and why some people survive destructive parent/child relationships while others are destroyed. He then connects this theme to a larger examination of the nature of evil and how the innocence of childhood becomes transformed in our society by the complex adult world of greed and cruelty. The traditional stories King presents form a bridge between the world of the child and the world of the adult. While some of these stories belong to children, others are appreciated by adults who have not lost the power of the imagination they had when they were young. The way King combines these stories reflects his view of the horror genre and what it reveals about society.

Of the fairy tales mentioned in *The Shining*, some are more important than others for understanding the novel's themes. We can see the whole novel as a version of the nursery rhyme about Jack and Jill, with references to the mountain and Jack's fall. The rhyme gives no reason for Jack's fall, and we don't know if Jack and Jill are permanently damaged. Wendy's first visit to the huge kitchen in the Overlook contains references to Hansel and Gretel. " 'I think I'll have to leave a trail of breadcrumbs every time I come in,' she said" (72). The evil in this tale comes from the parents, who send their children into the forest. The father, on the advice of his new wife, tries to rid himself of his children. Wendy walks next to Hallorann, while Jack and Danny hang back. If the Overlook Hotel is the castle of fairy tales, the kitchen is definitely its storehouse. The lists of food Hallorann describes to Wendy make us think of a giant's feast. But the ovens recall the witch who wants to cook Hansel. The kitchen, like everything else in the hotel, is too much for a small family. We share Wendy's feelings of being overwhelmed. But this kitchen does not really belong to the wicked witch. It is Hallorann's place in the hotel. And all he asks of Wendy is to keep it clean. King later tells us that the Torrances decide to eat in the kitchen rather than in the hotel dining room. Hansel and Gretel survive by fooling the witch. Wendy shoves Jack into the pantry much as Gretel stuffs the witch into her own oven. But evil is not destroyed as easily in *The Shining*, because Grady opens the door for Jack. Jack does eventually die like the witch when the hotel burns. As in the story, the characters have to work together to destroy the evil.

Danny's fairy tale also has a happy ending. As he is drawn to room 217 for the first time, he remembers a story his daddy told him when he was three, one his mother thought was too horrible for such a young child. It is the story of Bluebeard's wife, who has the same corn-colored hair as his mother. She lives in a castle like the Overlook. And she, too, is curious about a locked room. When she finally opens it she finds the heads of Bluebeard's seven previous wives. When she tries to leave, Bluebeard tells her that she too will die because of her curiosity. Danny knows that the story has a happy ending, but he can't remember it (170).

When he finally does enter the room, the tale of Bluebeard's wife merges with two other stories in his mind. The jumble of images he experiences includes references to the ending of Little Red Riding Hood, popular sayings such as "curiosity killed the cat," and *Alice in Wonderland* (215–16). He mixes up two unreal worlds. *"is that a wolf in a* BLUEBEARD *suit or a* BLUEBEARD *in a wolf suit"* (215). The knowledge shared by children which should protect him is not effective in a world of adult evil he cannot really understand.

Most children in King's fiction are able to deal with monsters because they are extensions of childhood fantasies. The children have the imaginative ability to believe in the supernatural. Here the horror is too real and too extreme. The images from *Alice in Wonderland* are mixed up with Danny's vision of the future. The Red Queen's croquet party turns into Jack's attack with the roque mallet. When Danny finally opens the door to room 217, he sees the suicide. The description of her is strangely adult even though it is supposed to be from Danny's point of view. "Her breasts lolled. Her pubic hair floated. Her hands were frozen on the knurled porcelain sides of the tub like claws" (217). The horror in the hotel seems to present Danny with an adult view of the world. Childhood beliefs cannot save him from his father. His childhood has given him conflicting evidence about his father's character. His father may be the good father associated with positive images of the family or the evil father of fairy tales. He survives when he learns to tell the difference between the real and the fairy tale. Hallorann has told him that the images in the hotel are not real. But he knows he can't deny them. He sees behind the mask. "It was not his daddy, not this Saturday Night Shock Show horror with its rolling eyes and hunched and hulking shoulders and blood-drenched shirt" (426). Once he can deny his father, Jack emerges for a moment from the monster he has become to tell Danny to run away. Danny recognizes and reconciles with his father by kissing one of his bloody hands. The kind of evil which takes over his father is unlike Danny's fairy tales. Danny's ability to see into the future and into the minds of adults places him in a world of his own.

The story connected with the Overlook Hotel is part of the adult world. "The Masque of the Red Death" criticizes the wealthy who attempt to avoid the plague by isolating themselves in a castle. They dance while outside people die. In the end death finds them. The Overlook echoes with ghosts who ride the elevator to the masked ball featured on an invitation Jack finds in an old scrapbook. The ball is thrown by Horace Derwent, a millionaire with ties to the Mafia. He tries to isolate his guests from the world. But as they all learn, isolation leads to evil. Derwent's past features a mythic rise from poverty to wealth accompanied by rumors that his business dealings were not always legitimate. While the events in "The Masque of the Red Death" happen only once, the ghosts of the Overlook have infected the hotel with their evil. They have become part of the hotel and haunt it with recurring manifestations of their traumatic past events.

To King the greed of adults leads them to destroy the world of childhood and innocence. Jack tells the story of Bluebeard before Danny is ready for such an introduction to the world of grown-ups. Wendy sees the connection between the two worlds, but she finds out that fairy tales do not hold up to the adult stories contained in the Overlook. When she tries to lock the evil father in the pantry, a ghost frees him. Danny must learn how to connect the two worlds to survive. Hallorann helps him understand that the world does not work the way fairy tales do. People do not necessarily live happily ever after. "The world's a hard place, Danny. It don't care" (446). The important thing is to go on. Danny's special powers bring him to danger and help him to escape. The hotel tries to get him, but his new father tells him stories which help save him. In the end he, his mother, and Hallorann live because Danny remembers something his fathers and the ghosts have forgotten, the pressure in the boiler. The explosion which comes from the real world is finally able to destroy the world of ghosts.

## ALTERNATE READING: FEMINISM

A feminist reading of a work may use many different methods to examine women's issues in a text. Because such a reading may examine how power operates in the novel, one approach is to look at the plot structure to see which character controls the action. Much of the concern feminists have about women's roles relates to the extent to which women can act freely rather than being dominated by others. Feminist criticism also offers a perspective on the roles women play in literature. Such an approach analyzes women's images and the author's attitude toward them. The horror genre is notorious for its presentation of women as powerless victims. A feminist analysis of a horror novel would examine both how the women are characterized and how their actions are presented. King's early horror fiction demonstrates problems with both types of readings. He has trouble portraying women realistically, and his women often react more than they act.

Another horror novelist, Chelsea Quinn Yarbro, observes a flaw in King's exploration of both issues in *The Shining*. "It is disheartening when a writer with so much talent and strength and vision is not able to develop a believable woman character between the ages of seventeen and sixty" (*Fear Itself* 49). King's early novels do not often have balanced images of women, although many of his later novels deal with issues related to women's lives in more complex ways. As Yarbro points out, Wendy doesn't do much in the novel. She just reacts to situations once they are critical. She is presented as a good wife trapped in an abusive relationship. Jack reflects extensively on his childhood and his father; Wendy is only briefly shown in connection with her mother.

One of Jack's excuses for not leaving the hotel is that the only place they can go is to Wendy's mother, who has never liked him. Wendy's mother is a stereotype of the mother who takes over her child. And Wendy is afraid of becoming her mother. Wendy is both mother and child. Like Gretel's stepmother in the story, Wendy's mother threw her out of the house. Her mother blamed Wendy for her divorce. But Wendy's mother is a much less significant character than Jack's father. King places women in traditional roles with traditional lives. He does not give us enough information to understand Wendy's mother and her choices. We do not know why she acts as she does. We learn little about the lives of these two women apart from their connections with their husbands or children. Even though King is aware of the abuse that can go on in relationships, in his early fiction women tend to contribute to their own abuse.

Jack's break with his father comes when he is nine years old. His father beats his mother with a cane, just as Jack will later beat Wendy. King portrays both women as unable to act. King does not provide us with any insight into Jack's mother's immobility. Jack sees his mother's passivity as one of the causes of his father's behavior. Jack never frees himself from his father's influence, just as Danny finds it so hard to give up his relationship with Jack. But the women are never shown to have close connections. Wendy never has a positive moment with her mother. King accepts the repetitive patterns of mother-daughter relationships while reserving special interactions for fathers and sons. Wendy remembers how Jack took care of Danny when he was a baby, but we see no similar scenes with female characters.

While men may take on nontraditional roles in *The Shining*, the female characters stay fixed in expected positions. Jack's father is a male nurse, but none of the mothers work. The woman who commits suicide in the hotel lives off her husband and uses his money to buy herself a lover. Wendy follows Jack to the hotel because she is expected to obey her husband's wishes. Her failure to react quickly to Jack's disintegrating character is tied to her role as a traditional woman. Especially in horror fiction, women are more often victims than heroes.

Men are not entirely immune from stereotyping either. Feminism shows that when one group is not treated equally, the group in power is forced into traditional roles as well. All the violence in the novel is associated with the men. The gangsters shoot each other; Jack's attack with the mallet is described in great detail. Jack does all of the paid work, while Wendy cooks their meals. Even Wendy's one attempt to kill Jack is not successful. Women are not as good at violence as men. The men are also the drinkers, the alcoholics, the people who beat others when they are drunk. Men seem to have a greater potential for evil. The ghosts who draw Jack into the world of the hotel are men.

In a world where women's concerns are ignored, other groups may also suffer. Feminist critics also examine the treatment of minorities in fiction. King acknowledges that he stereotypes African Americans in his early novels. Hallorann does have a heroic role, but we never see him as an individual. At times it seems that King overcompensates for his inability to make African Americans realistic characters by making them heroes. Wendy is unable to act to save herself and her son, and Hallorann must return to the hotel to save them. Hallorann almost seems incidental to the novel at the beginning, where his function is to provide information about Danny's special sight. At the end of the novel King shows the survivors healing, but neither Wendy nor Hallorann seems to have changed as a result of their experiences. Danny will grow and change, but they remain static.

Older women are particularly unattractive in the world of this novel. The suicide is ugly and old when Danny sees her in the bathtub. A woman presents the last problem for the hotel when she checks out. She is described as "a dreadnought of a woman bundled into a long fur coat and what looked like a feather boa" (66). She is also loud. These women also represent wealth which they have done nothing to earn. Wealth is associated with power, but women use the power that comes with wealth without earning it. They are also shown using their power in petty ways, like intimidating hotel employees. The wealthy men in *The Shining* may be evil, but they also are a part of the American dream.

Derwent is an inventor, a businessman, a gangster, and a film producer, what we like to call a self-made man. We admire much of what he does even if we do not approve of his methods. The women in this novel never share any of this kind of power.

Later in his career King finds ways to make interesting, independent women of all ages come alive in his novels. But in *The Shining*, as in much of his early work, they are little more than cardboard figures who are necessary to the plot but have little individuality or life of their own. In these early novels King begins to find his own approach to the horror genre. He expands on traditional elements of the ghost story, like the terror associated with the moving topiary figures, by adding such elements of the modern world as snowmobiles. He explores the complexity of Jack's character. But at this point in his career he adopts without alteration the horror genre's view of women.

5

# *The Stand* (1978)

*The Stand* is one of King's most popular novels. Although it was originally published in 1978, many of the concerns it raises about American society are even more relevant today. Many people still mistrust the government's experiments with chemicals and believe in the possibility of an accident which could destroy us. We are concerned about what happens when small groups of people create their own social structures and choose what we consider to be the wrong approach to organizing society. As in King's novella "The Langoliers," published in *Four Past Midnight*, the idea of a small band of survivors who are the last people in the world is fascinating. We all would like to know how and why the characters respond and consider how we might react in such a world. We also wonder if we would survive in similar circumstances.

King cut 400 manuscript pages before publishing the first edition of *The Stand*. The preface to the complete edition published in 1990 claims that the original version was shortened because of economic considerations. The new edition has an additional 150,000 words. King updates the time of the novel from the 1980s to the 1990s and adds short chapters at the beginning and end. The new version also contains black and white illustrations by Bernie Wrightson. I will discuss the complete version of *The Stand*. I personally like the additional information about the characters and such episodes as Trashcan Man's encounter with The Kid, which is left out of the first edition.

Some critics feel that, in addition to adding information about characters and detailing the course of the superflu, which sets the plot in motion, King shifts the tone of the novel in the complete version. Edwin F. Casebeer suggests that the three main sections of the novel more clearly fall into different genres in the original version. Casebeer sees the first section of *The Stand* as part of the science fiction genre because it keeps its realistic tone. Science fiction tries to place its view of the future in a realistic framework. The second section provides a transition from science fiction to the epic fantasy of the last section. In epic fantasy characters face challenging situations in an imaginary world which can be very different from our own. The complete version of *The Stand* introduces the fantasy elements much earlier (Magistrale, *Dark Descent* 49). Fantasy works are based on magical or supernatural events which are not part of our everyday realistic world.

Many people have tried to decide in what genre the novel best fits. Its epic quest structure is similar to J. R. R. Tolkien's *The Lord of the Rings*, where a small band sets out on a search which results in a confrontation with evil. The idea of the small group on a quest is explored in several different ways in King's novel. *The Stand* traces the journeys of various people who try to find the means to come together and survive during and after the plague. The book also contains many fantasy elements. Fantasy literature can be magical without horrifying the reader. While we generally think of fantasy as taking place in some undefined past, King combines elements of fantasy with a realistic setting associated with science fiction.

King's mixture of genres is present in both versions of the novel. They both clearly begin as science fiction when the plague is released, and we follow its results. The first sections also show events with realistic sources which challenge existing social structures. Such episodes are typical of science fiction. Perhaps the best way to consider the mixture of genres is to think of the novel as an example of apocalyptic fiction, a genre which can include science fiction, horror, and fantasy. Apocalyptic literature usually deals with major events which reveal great truths connected to concerns about the end of the world as we know it. King contrasts the world before and after the apocalypse to measure who and what we are and what we might become.

## PLOT DEVELOPMENT AND NARRATIVE STRUCTURE

*The Stand* is King's most elaborate novel. It covers a great deal of territory and has a large number of characters. King works through the introduction and development of these characters, their movements across the United States, and their formation of new groups in the major sections of the novel. At the same time the novel is shaped almost like a giant funnel. We go from a huge number of important characters at the beginning to the hero, the heroine, and their child at the end.

King does an amazing job of organization in *The Stand*. Aside from the opening and closing chapters, *The Stand* is divided into three books. These books are further divided into chapters of varying lengths, which are numbered consecutively. Each book deals with a longer period of time—from days in the first book to several months in the third book. Even though the opening chapter is not specifically included in the time scheme of the novel, we know that it immediately precedes the dates and title given for the first book: "Captain Trips/June 16-July 4, 1990" (xx). Captain Trips is the name given to the superflu, which has a 99.4 percent infection rate and no cure (Captain Trips is also a nickname for the late Jerry Garcia of The Grateful Dead).

The first book of *The Stand* also alternates the introduction of survivors with stories of those who die from Captain Trips. King ties pieces of information to significant events so that we can remember each individual. These characters gradually interact as they slowly begin their movement west. The first book ends on July 4 for two reasons. The Fourth of July holiday is an ironic contrast to the actual condition of the United States at this point in the novel. The government which created the plague and committed horrible acts to protect people from knowledge of it no longer exists. The date is also important because by now only those who are immune are left alive. The dates help us follow the progress of the fatal flu as it makes its way across the country. King varies the amount of time between chapters and the amount of time each chapter covers. In the beginning he often includes the time as well as the date to give a sense of how quickly the events rush along. Charlie, the original transmitter of the plague, dies at ten after nine on June 16. He has taken his family and escaped from the military base which is the source of the plague. His movement across the country from the western California desert to Stu Redman in Texas is the initial track of the spread of the deadly disease. But the chapter which deals with this event also introduces Stu, the hero of the story. He immediately stands out from the other men at the gas station because he has the sense to turn off the gas tanks before Charlie's car crashes into them.

The second chapter introduces Fran Goldsmith, the heroine, and her failing relationship with her boyfriend, Jess. At first we think that details like Fran's connection to Jess or the information about the other men at the gas station are important. As people begin to die, we quickly realize how unimportant such relationships are in the face of life and death struggles. King alternates between the personal and the larger picture. He uses Starkey, who commands the army's attempt to contain the disaster, and the doctors who treat the early victims to give us a sense of the scope and speed of the disease's spread. The next few chapters introduce the rest of the important characters. Once the secondary characters die, we can tell what is going to happen. King does not try to surprise us by killing off anyone he has made interesting. While we may not guess the scope of the disease at the beginning, it does not take us long to realize that it will not be contained. The army's effort will not succeed, and we know the statistics for its communicability from the top secret papers on Starkey's desk.

King uses a shifting point of view to introduce characters and events. He often takes us right into the thoughts and dreams of the central characters. He is more objective with many of the others' deaths. Sometimes he seems to talk to us. He shows how the disease spreads from Arnette, Texas, by tracing its passage from a policeman to an insurance salesman to tourists. He then tells about chain letters, which usually don't work. In an ironic tone he tells how well this particular chain letter does work. "This one, the Captain Trips chain letter, worked very well. The pyramid was indeed being built not from the bottom up but from the tip down—said tip being a deceased army security guard named Charles Campion" (73). He continues to track the disease, and his tone contrasts with the events. We are pulled along by the rapid progress of the events.

We have little time to think about the consequences of all of this death before King turns our attention to destruction. By moving from big cities to small towns, we realize how quickly civilization breaks down. But the survivors outside big population areas are safer. They must deal with the loss of family members, but they don't face the looting and shooting Larry Underwood sees in New York. In all situations the survivors feel the need to move on. King gives them a goal, which is suggested by the conflicting dreams they begin to experience. They gradually begin to locate the place and the person they must find. They also dream of the walking dude, Randall Flagg. As readers we get only small amounts of information to begin with, but from our knowledge of many different characters' dreams we can put the pieces together more quickly than they can. We begin to get a sense of the pattern King is developing. By the end of the first book, most of the main characters have been introduced and are beginning to meet each other.

The second book gradually unites the central characters into two groups, good and evil, associated with three locations: Hemingford Home, Boulder, and Las Vegas. The dreams lead many of the characters to Mother Abagail in Hemingford Home, Nebraska. These dreams often alternate with nightmares of the dark man. We meet Mother Abagail, the last important character to be introduced. King also introduces a new source of information about the characters. Both Fran and Harold Lauder keep journals. Fran records how she feels, what has happened, and things to remember. As the groups begin to form new societies, we see the contrast between our world and theirs. We are fascinated by the problems they encounter and the solutions they find. King adds further tension by introducing personality conflicts that will lead to confrontations. We are never easy with Harold and wait for him to react when he learns of the relationship between Fran and Stu.

King also continues to develop certain characters who remain outsiders even when they do join a group. Trashcan Man leaves a trail of fire behind him. He only wants to serve Flagg, but once they meet, King foreshadows their destruction with a single sentence. Flagg tells Trashcan Man he is going to set him burning things. The chapter ends with frightening words: "And in the end, that burning was very great" (627). As the two groups build their new worlds, King also intensifies the tensions between them and their opposing communities in Boulder and Las Vegas. The group under Flagg's leadership in Las Vegas plans further destruction. In Boulder those who followed Mother Abagail form a governing committee and send out spies to find out what Flagg is doing.

The first real conflict between the two groups comes from within. Harold, the traitor, plants the bomb which kills Nick, a deaf mute. Harold is assisted by Nadine, who is drawn to Flagg. While Nick is not the first to die since the plague, his is the first significant death, the first to suggest the real complexity of setting up a new society. Nick is one of the moral and ethical cores of the community. King builds up to the explosion, forcing us to guess when Harold will press the button and who will survive. We move beyond the violence and death to the end of Mother Abagail and the beginning of the final quest. She sends four men and a dog on a journey to Las Vegas. She cannot see the end of this voyage, but she knows that they must go. "God didn't bring you folks together to make a committee or a community. . . . He brought you here only to send you further, on a quest" (917). But the connections the four men who must leave have made within the community, and the mystical intermingling of their thoughts that has already taken place, mean that the four are more than they seem. They may be individuals, but they are also part of a whole. Mother Abagail tells them that Nick is not totally gone. She also tells them that if one of them falls on the quest, the next man must take over for him. The second section ends with the men on the road. They must go by foot and leave everything behind as they move into the mythic space of their quest.

The final book of *The Stand* does not begin with the quest. It follows those who have gone toward Las Vegas as spies. King continues gradually eliminating most of the central characters. We move from the death of a judge, whom we get to know only briefly, to Harold, whom we have been following since the beginning. At the same time Nadine moves toward Flagg. But their union leads to her death. She and Harold provide the connection between the two worlds of Randall Flagg and Mother Abagail, but they never fit in either one.

At this point many things happen at the same time. Trashcan Man heads out into the desert. Tom Cullen, one of the spies, manages to escape from Las Vegas after he is recognized and heads back toward Boulder. Their travels purify the men from Boulder for their quest. Trashcan Man is also purified, but not from natural sources. He is a victim of the radiation emitted by his prize possession, the atom bomb he finds and takes back to Flagg. The confrontation we anticipate is not the real end of *The Stand*. The men from Boulder do make their own personal and collective stands against Flagg in Las Vegas. While three of them are consumed by the atomic explosion that destroys this community, Stu, who has been left behind with Kojak, the dog, returns with the help of Tom. Tom is not alone either. Nick appears to him and tells him how to save Stu. These events would seem to tell us that we need other people to survive. But King continues beyond the heroics of the group and individuals to the birth of Fran's child, the real test of whether life will continue. We might expect this affirmation to end the novel, but Stu and Fran make a final stand when they decide to leave Boulder and return to Maine.

We see only the beginning of their journey. The novel ends not with a resolution but with a new set of questions. Stu and Fran's decision to get away from the same old problems which arise whenever people live together makes us wonder again about what we might do. Unlike the traditional horror novel, which ends with the destruction of evil, this work has an open ending. We assume that Stu, Fran, and the baby will survive, but we don't know. The chapter King has added to the complete edition makes the ending even more ambiguous. Here Flagg does not just disappear in Las Vegas; he awakens and finds himself in the jungle with a tribe whose language he does not speak. He introduces himself as Russell Faraday, another one of his names, and tells them he has come to teach them to be civilized. If Fran and Stu's chapter ends with their questioning whether people ever learn, Flagg's suggests that they will repeat the same mistakes over and over. "Life was such a wheel that no man could stand upon it for long. And it always, at the end, came round to the same place again" (1153). We are left to make the decision. Who has the right answer? We have seen Flagg's defeat. But we also know that Fran and Stu leave the civilization they have created. The end of the novel makes us question how we can live and whether we should live together or apart.

## CHARACTERS

The characters in *The Stand* can be placed in three groups: the basically good people with Mother Abagail Freemantle as the ideal, the basically evil with Randall Flagg as the extreme, and those who combine good and evil, some finally choosing one direction and some the other. The characters at either extreme remain static, while those in the middle show the greatest change. Because there are so many major characters, we will examine only the most important members of each group.

### The Good Characters

The largest number of characters in *The Stand* fall into the good category. They congregate in Boulder and work together to establish that community. Most are introduced early in the first book of the novel. But King does not bring in Mother Abagail until much later. Some have criticized King's characterization of this 108-year-old African American woman as stereotypical. She does exhibit some character traits associated with people of her age and cultural background. But it could also be argued that King runs counter to stereotypes by not making the most Godlike character a white male. While King does give her individualizing touches such as her father's involvement with the Grange, an organization not usually associated with African Americans, she still remains a rather stereotyped character. King's general criticism of what has gone wrong with the United States extends to its past with the story of Mother Abagail's life.

The single episode King uses to define her childhood involves her tremendous success singing at the Grange talent show. Her first dream of Flagg repeats this experience but with much different results. All of her fears about the event recur during the dream. Her next encounter with Flagg's evil, after she returns with a chicken from a neighboring farm to feed the people who are coming to see her, is more serious. The dark man sends weasels to attack her, but her faith and courage save her. The weasels disappear, but she still feels the dark man's eye on her. From this introduction we learn all we need to know about Mother Abagail. We see her strengths and how she overcomes her weaknesses. We associate her goodness with traditional values and religion. She and the other good characters work toward a certain balance with the natural world. The characters who come to her have visions of the cornfield, a cultivated natural world. She cries when she looks at the corn and knows that there will be no one to harvest it. She respects the land and what it gives us when we live in harmony with it.

Nick Andros is the closest to Mother Abagail on a goodness scale. Nick is one of her guests in Nebraska, and she recognizes his potential. Unlike those who have to divorce themselves from their possessions before they can confront Flagg, Nick has never really had anything. He is able to talk and hear only after his death, and he is the first central character to die. He is also the first leader of the group in Boulder. If Mother Abagail dies after her job is finished, Nick dies as a martyr who inspires the others.

Stu Redman and Fran Goldsmith can also be seen as representing certain stereotypes. Stuart's name suggests his role as a kind of everyman, a combination of Native American and European ancestors. Fran seems to be a typical college student who is still part of a nuclear family. She loves her parents but can be independent of them. Stu's background places him among those who still would like to participate in the American Dream, even though circumstances have prevented him from doing so. His father, a dentist, died when Stu was young, and Stu finally had to give up dreams of a college athletic scholarship to support his brother.

We know that he is quick thinking because he is the one who shuts down the gas pumps before Charlie's crash. We find out more about him when he is the subject of investigation because of his immunity to the plague. We follow his actions and admire his decisions, his honesty, and the way he treats people. Even when he breaks his leg on the way to Las Vegas and almost gives up, we still believe in him.

We have a similar view of Fran. She, too, represents stability. King has carefully developed the character of the woman who will bear the first child in his new world. But both she and Stu react in predictable ways to events. Fran doesn't want Stu to leave her to finish the quest. She gets angry at Mother Abagail for suggesting it. While she is one of two women on the ad hoc governing committee, she does spend a certain amount of time supporting her man. Women do perform important actions, but they are not as fully developed as the male characters.

## The Evil Characters

Just as Mother Abagail is the measure of good in *The Stand,* Randall Flagg is representative of extreme evil. But he does not have the kind of history or personality we see in Mother Abagail. He takes many shapes in the novel. He is the dark man, the walking dude, the shape shifter, the man of many names. He appears as a crow watching the other characters. His pockets are full of pamphlets for all types of causes. He is identified as one who supports the more radical elements of society, such as the Klan, the cop killer, the anti-Semite. He has connections to serial killers, presidential assassins, and political radicals. Flagg is reborn or transfigured when times change (183–84). He first appears in the natural world and has connections with wild animals. But his real home is the technological community he sets up in Las Vegas. The people he leads manage to restore the world which generated the plague. He wants planes and bombs to attack the Boulder community. Flagg admires the savage aspects of the natural world, but he needs people to accomplish his goals.

The other major evil characters are introduced in the midst of actions which establish their character. Lloyd Henreid and his buddy Andrew "Poke" Freeman have already killed six people when we first meet them. Lloyd has just come out of prison after serving time for attempted rape and reconnects with Poke, his former cellmate. The first thing they do is betray a friend and kill him. They are small time crooks who generate a big time manhunt. There is never any doubt that Lloyd will serve Flagg. They meet when Flagg saves him from starvation in prison. All of the guards are victims of the flu, and Lloyd is ready to eat his dead cellmate when Flagg frees him. Like the rest of the members of Flagg's community, Lloyd gains power from his association with the dark man, but his character does not change.

Most of the other men and women who join Flagg fall into the recognizable stereotypes one would expect to find around Las Vegas. The only people generally considered good are the police and members of the military, who are attracted to Flagg's totalitarian organization of the community. Their presence is not really that unexpected since we associate these careers with people who like a strictly regulated society. We also get the sense that they do not fully appreciate Flagg's evil or that they prefer to see him as only doing what needs to be done to maintain order.

## The Characters in the Middle

Three of the most interesting characters in the novel are torn between good and evil: Harold Lauder, Larry Underwood, and Nadine Cross. Nadine is the least complex of the three. She fights the attraction of Flagg, but she comes under his control because of her sexual desires. She does have the occasional good impulse, such as when she saves Joe, the young boy. Nadine also serves as a connection between Larry and Harold because she establishes a relationship with both of them. When Larry meets her and the boy attacks him, Larry has his first realization that he has changed into a better human being because he cares about these people. Nadine's relationship with Harold focuses his anger into the creation of the bomb which kills Nick. But Nadine is not evil enough to survive Flagg. Their sexual union destroys her. She responds by committing suicide and killing the child she is carrying. She is one of the examples of Flagg's failure when she destroys his future offspring.

Harold and Larry reflect King's personal concerns as well as showing how characters resolve personality conflicts in the world ruled by Captain Trips. Many people see elements of the young King in Harold, the awkward adolescent. The ability to transform life into art saves King and Larry Underwood. Harold's inability to grow up and control his bitterness destroys him. He, too, wants to write; he appreciates the power of words. But Harold doesn't have the moral strength to become an artist. He comes closest to his true nature in his death. Flagg arranges his accident. Harold accepts it and is finally able to act when he kills himself.

Larry's character is the one most in doubt during the novel. Larry and King both must deal with sudden success. King wrote *The Stand* when he "was suffering from a really good case of career jet lag" (*Danse Macabre* 372). Larry almost destroys himself before the plague strikes. Once he realizes that the world has changed and that fame and money are no longer important, he grows stronger. He makes good decisions. Larry is heroic in death because he is able to face his fears. He is able to face the crowd in Las Vegas and tell them why Flagg is killing them: "We're being put to death because Randall Flagg is afraid of us" (1079). He even manages to break through to some of those who watch. The response of Whitney Horgan forces Flagg to release the ball of fire which ultimately sets off the atom bomb. We see Larry's death as a triumph because we have followed his journey from what he was to what he has become. We are happy to see someone choose the right path.

## THEME

King develops four major themes in *The Stand*: the role of traditional institutions in our lives; the relationship between the individual and society; interactions between individuals; and the moral dilemmas faced by each person. King works out these themes through his development of both characters and events. He is concerned with how we come together to form a social order, the value of such a community, and interaction between the individual and society. He wants to see if we can find a balance between order and chaos and if it is possible for good to triumph over evil. Each theme presents a stand taken in the face of an attack. In some cases the stand is positive; good wins over evil. But some of the stands lead to destruction and the triumph of evil.

The first section of the novel focuses on the role of traditional organizations which control our lives, such as the government, the military, and the scientific establishment. King suggests that our institutions are no longer responsible to those who created them. An event like the plague could occur because none of these societal structure really care about the people they are supposed to serve. The spread of the superflu results from poor security, and mistakes are made in handling the virus, but King questions the need for the scientific research which produces the plague and for organizations that end up executing the people they are supposed to protect.

King's attitude toward science is typical of the horror genre, which often questions the role of science. But in the horror genre the mad scientist's experiments do not usually threaten the structure of society. The mad scientist often ignores the law because knowledge is more important. Victor Frankenstein creates his monster because he is testing the connections between life and death. In *The Stand* the scientists are not trying to expand our understanding of the universe, they are just looking for a new way to kill the enemies of the United States. The images we see of the dead scientists show that they have not died in heroic positions. They have avoided taking a stand until it is too late. They develop the superflu because it is part of their job. They never question the need for such a virus. Their failure to take a stand leads to the destruction of their world.

But if the scientists are just ordinary people doing assigned jobs, the military is more sinister. They take drastic measures to attempt to control the spread of the plague and do not hesitate to kill those who stand in their way. They are frightening because they feel that their actions are necessary to save society. King questions whether such a society is worth saving. The stand the military takes is too extreme, attempting to control the spread of the disease as though they are fighting a battle. King shows that this attitude is doomed to failure because military force is not the correct response to this crisis. The secrecy the military maintains only creates a greater desire to know. The force they use generates resistance. The military's stand results in more deaths because force and control are the only means they have of dealing with the threat of the plague.

People normally turn to the government in times of crisis. King shows us that the government's only response is to resort to force. When even the military's effort breaks down, citizens are left on their own. By placing characters in a variety of locations King explores the different ways society disintegrates. While individuals in smaller communities seem to be safest during the spread of the plague, King suggests that any extreme can be dangerous. Lloyd almost dies alone in prison when all of his jailers get the plague. Stu avoids a similar fate in a research facility where he has been taken for observation. While Randall Flagg helps Lloyd escape, Stu manages on his own. Once these men escape from their prisons they return to a very different world. Lloyd knows he must serve the dark man, but Stu has to discover his destiny. Larry faces the effects of the plague in the middle of a large city, New York. In the city, violence is one of the first effects of the breakdown of order. But Larry soon finds that the remains of civilization make it hard to leave the city. Cars and bodies fill the streets. One of the most frightening experiences in the novel is Larry's trip through the darkness of the Lincoln Tunnel as he exits the city. When he loses his lighter, Larry almost goes mad because he can no longer avoid bumping into bodies.

Gradually, those who are left come together to form new social groups. The novel becomes more pessimistic as people fall back into the same patterns which created the plague. In Las Vegas the desire for order leads to a dictatorship. The same partnership of technology and science which developed the superflu works to destroy their enemies in Boulder. Flagg almost succeeds because he provides the order and control some people need. He gives other people the enemy they crave and the evil atmosphere they find attractive. The ad hoc committee tries to find a way to implement democracy in Boulder. But by the end of the novel old social orders begin to reassert themselves. The deputies in Boulder have guns.

Stu sees these moves toward a more formal society as the beginning of the same old tensions. He hopes that more time and distance will help people learn from their mistakes. He wants the few survivors of the plague to spread out across the United States to prevent too much organization. He also hopes to be able to teach his son to avoid the mistakes that have brought humans so close to self-destruction. At the end of the novel Stu, Fran, and the baby have reached Mother Abagail's house on their return to Maine. Stu's actions inspire others who are interested in leaving the Free Zone in Boulder. Stu and his new family have worked through the day-to-day problems of living. But they do not have answers to the most basic question: they don't know if people can really learn from their mistakes. Stu makes his stand by leaving Boulder. Others make a stand when they sacrifice themselves for the Colorado community.

In addition to examining the operation of society in a crisis, King uses the superflu as a way to see how individuals react in these conditions. While we are often disappointed at how society operates in *The Stand*, we are pleased with the ways some individuals deal with the plague. Many reactions to the almost universal death are predictable. Some people refuse to believe they may die. Some spread the plague through ignorance, others because they don't realize they are infected. Some die poorly, and some die well. Each victim also takes a stand in the face of death.

Those who remain after the superflu has run its course become more individualized in their responses to the world and to each other. While some stereotypes remain, many people look for a new way to live. Some form small groups in order to attack weaker individuals. But many people help each other out. In some small groups the weak are protected, and any life is considered important. While emotional responses remain the same, some individuals become more heroic. Individuals meet other survivors. Some people become more generous and giving as a result of their experiences. Others become even more mean and jealous than they were before. The survivors split into two groups. Until each group forms a new community, we follow people who are trying to discover how to live in this new world. Nick finds Tom Cullen, a mentally handicapped man who can't read what Nick writes when they try to communicate. But they manage to understand each other. Harold's one-sided love of Fran turns into jealousy, which finally consumes him when he learns of her relationship with Stu.

The survivors have few problems with the basics of existence. Aside from highways, which are often blocked by cars whose occupants died on the road, the whole world of material goods is open to them. Their interactions with other survivors are free of some of the usual problems we face. While these small groups may lack people with critical skills, like doctors or mechanics, they do not need to deal with greed or envy of each other's possessions. Just as life is taken down to its basics, emotions also become simplified. But some of the emotions which remain cause old problems to reemerge. King shows how basic human nature is the source of much of the pain in our relationships with each other. If we cannot rid ourselves of negative emotions, we cannot change the way we treat each other.

King realizes that circumstances may give people reasons to reevaluate their lives, but he also knows that change must come from within the individual. Larry's experiences change him from a self-involved fame seeker to a person willing to die so that the rest of the community can survive. Harold only becomes more bitter as his early insecurity turns into jealousy and hatred. The survivors are drawn to good or evil—Flagg or Mother Abagail. But although Flagg and Mother Abagail may influence the paths some people take, ultimately people must make their own choices. While good may triumph at the end of the novel, King knows that evil will also reappear to provide new challenges. As long as human nature remains constant, it will be difficult for us to change by learning from the past.

In *The Stand* people begin their journey by going from east to west.

They are retracing the mythic past of the United States, following the pioneers. King knows that these myths of the conquering of the West along with the story of the Pilgrims are central to our understanding of what makes us Americans. These are stories of people overcoming odds to create new lives. But by the 1980s people began to question these myths. As Stuart Redman's name suggests, such myths can be destructive as well as constructive. If Stu's journey west is over the bodies of those who have died by the plague, our ancestors walked over the bodies of people who already lived on the land. Mother Abagail's story reminds us of another part of our past that is often forgotten. Slavery and racism are also part of our history. Stu and Fran try to erase this history by going back, by traveling in the opposite direction. They see their hope for a new world in retracing their steps, remembering their past. One of Fran's journals entries lists things which should not be forgotten. King knows there are no easy answers to these questions about the future of the United States and how we should deal with our past. By ending *The Stand* with the rebirth of Flagg, he also suggests that certain conflicts will never end. Even if we can learn, Flagg will always be there to challenge us.

## ALTERNATE READING: RELIGIOUS IMAGES

In the introduction to the expanded version of *The Stand*, King calls the novel "this long dark tale of Christianity" (xii). Apocalyptic fiction, which deals with events leading to the end of the world as we know it, lends itself to the use of religious imagery. The term "apocalypse" is associated with the idea of revelation in the Judeo-Christian tradition. The ultimate conflict in *The Stand* is between good and evil. One way to look at *The Stand* is to examine how King uses religious symbolism to express its central conflict. While King claims a moral framework for his fiction, he does not seem to be interested in its religious impact. "Morality is, after all, a codification of those things which the heart understands to be true and those things which the heart understands to be the demands of a life lived among others . . . civilization, in a word." He does not want to connect morality to "ridiculous posturing" (*Danse* 375). As we look at the symbols King uses, we need to ask ourselves how these symbols are used, who they are associated with, and what they mean in the novel.

Most of the Christian imagery in *The Stand* is associated with the two characters who represent the extremes of good and evil, Randall Flagg and Mother Abagail. She lives the ideal Christian life. The Christian images surrounding her are associated with her actions. Her entire life is an example of the power of Christianity. King introduces Flagg as a generalized presence. He lives an evil life, but his power is communicated to others through symbols. His appearance in the novel is connected to images of rebirth of a monster. Starkey explains to Creighton, who is taking over for him, how to make certain the plague spreads to the enemies of the United States through our agents in China and the U.S.S.R. He talks about the poems of William Butler Yeats and recalls the line from "The Second Coming" about how things fall apart. He has memorized the last line, about the beast slouching toward Bethlehem to be born. This reference comes right before the chapter introducing Flagg.

From this initial image Flagg is associated with symbols of destruction. Contact with Flagg inverts the traditional meanings of these symbols. Those who join him share these perverted images. Religions present plagues as warnings to humans of the evil in their lives. Flagg sees the plague as the signal for his rebirth, and Trashcan Man sees it as the fulfillment of his destiny. Flagg is associated with ideas of the cycle of life at the end of the novel. Trashcan Man is introduced as one "who has discovered the great axle of his destiny and has laid his hands upon it" (298). But both men are interested only in destruction.

Flagg uses crucifixion as a punishment in Las Vegas. Just before we actually witness this punishment, we follow Trashcan Man as he approaches the city. He talks to a crow, convinced it is the dark man. King sees this as an example of religious mania, which "is one of the few infallible ways of responding to the world's vagaries, because it totally eliminates pure accident" (617). Trashcan Man, like Peter, refuses to recognize Hector Dragon three times while Hector is led to the cross. The notice of Hector's sin, drug abuse, is nailed to the cross above his head. Immediately after this act Trashcan Man goes to meet Flagg and repeats the words he has been saying over and over. "My . . . my life for you" (626). This kind of sacrifice is usually associated with good, but Trashcan Man wants to devote his life to Flagg. Ultimately Trashcan Man's great gift for Flagg leads to the destruction of his master's city. Trashcan Man provides the cleansing fire, lit by the hand of God, which destroys Las Vegas. Fire is associated with the Judeo-Christian tradition both as a way for God to show himself and as a cleansing, destructive force. Trashcan Man does good by trying to support evil.

Mother Abagail is the strongest voice for a belief in forces beyond our understanding, and she locates these forces in a religious structure. When Stu dreams of her he hears a hymn from his childhood in the background (111). The dreams which bring the characters to Mother Abagail are contrasted with the signs Harold leaves behind to direct others. Harold is associated with technology and rationality, while dreams are associated with the unconscious mind. Mother Abagail does not use symbols or images to communicate. The characters dream of real events from her life. She appears as herself rather than through images. The first time we actually meet Mother Abagail she immediately sees the destruction as God's judgment (481). She accepts this judgment without question, using the story of Moses and the burning bush as her reason. Many of her reflections deal with her relationship with God and her understanding of this relationship. She knows that God does not care if she is afraid of the man with no face, Randall Flagg. She sees this man as just a little less powerful than God. She sees God directing her life, operating with some kind of master plan which has been in effect forever. She prepares a meal for those she knows are arriving. The meal is a common ritual of many religions and has many echoes in the Christian tradition.

The final quest of Glen Bateman, Stu Redman, Larry Underwood, and Ralph Brentner deals with ideas of faith and is religious in the sense that all quests recall the search for the Holy Grail. Glen says he will fear no evil when they talk about what will happen to them in Las Vegas. Even though Mother Abagail believes that God has told her that these men must go, they also find rational explanations for their journey. Glen associates the trip with the means used by Native Americans to achieve visions (1045). He also ties their experiences to those of the prophets who went off into the wilderness. Like these others who found peace in the desert, the three men are calm when they face their destiny in Las Vegas. Glen, who is the first to die, realizes the emptiness of Flagg. He calls Flagg "the last magician of rational thought" (1072), and he sees that Flagg is losing control.

Flagg's plan to kill the other two men recalls the Romans' methods of dealing with the early Christians. He is going to have them torn apart in front of the crowd he has forced to come and watch. Larry is finally at peace before the execution and accepts what is about to happen as God's plan, if there is a God. The false accusations Flagg reads before he sentences the two men also recall events of the Crucifixion. Ralph recognizes that the ball of fire Flagg has created is turning into the Hand of God. Larry thanks God as the bomb explodes. King ends the chapter with words filled with religious associations. "And the righteous and the unrighteous alike were consumed in that holy fire" (1085). The end of Las Vegas also recalls the destruction of the cities of the plain, Sodom and Gomorrah. King presents Las Vegas as a modern version of these two evil cities.

While religious symbols operate in *The Stand*, they do not seem to fall into a single pattern. The most traditional are associated with some of the most evil of the characters. Mother Abagail's faith is not based on image but on a belief that is honest and real in its appreciation of how God works. King does not like religious fundamentalism because he sees it as another version of the dictatorship Flagg establishes. He associates religious mania with destructive fanatics like Trashcan Man. He does believe in God, but he has concerns about organized religion (Underwood and Miller, *Feast* 64). His good characters can believe, but they do not have to create symbols to express their beliefs. His own attitude toward religion is mirrored in the way he uses its images. Religious symbols are props for the evil characters. Those who are good do not need religious imagery. They do not have to become saints for us to appreciate their morality.

# 6

# *The Dark Half* (1989)

Throughout his career Stephen King has explored the role of the writer. The adult hero of *'Salem's Lot* is a moderately successful author. As King has become a literary brand name (see Chapter 1), he has exhibited a growing concern about the role of the artist and the relationship of creator to audience and genre. The central member of the group which finally conquers the evil in *It* keeps in touch with his childhood because he is an author. In the realistic horror novel *Misery* (1987), King examines the extremes of the demands fans put on favorite authors by having a devoted reader of the romance genre attempt to take control of her favorite author's career. In *The Dark Half,* an author is trapped by his own creation. In this work King examines the connections between the horror and violent crime genres (see Alternate Reading, below). He also examines the conflict between money and art faced by the successful writer. The author must decide which is more important—writing to satisfy the public or oneself. King's final analysis of the author/work relationship occurs in the novella *Secret Window, Secret Garden,* which explores the interaction of author and character.

In *The Dark Half* King also works out his relationship to his pen name. From 1977 to 1984 he published five novels under the name Richard Bachman: *Rage, The Long Walk, Roadwork, The Running Man,* and *Thinner.* In his introduction to *The Bachman Books,* which collects four of these novels, King considers and rejects several explanations for becoming

Bachman, such as his publisher's request that he limit the number of his publications or an attempt to avoid being typecast as a horror novelist. He finds one possibility convincing: "I think I did it to turn the heat down a little bit; to do something as someone other than Stephen King" (viii). He was discovered as Bachman because the books were dedicated to people associated with his life and because one copyright form had his name. "Now people are asking me why I did it, and I don't seem to have any very satisfactory answers. Good thing I didn't murder anyone, isn't it?" (v). He discusses roleplaying by novelists and how he enjoyed being someone else for a while. He did develop a personality and biography for Bachman, who was depicted as not a very nice man. King had Bachman survive a brain tumor, but killed him off when the Bangor *Daily News* revealed his identity (vii).

In *The Dark Half* there are many parallels between Thad Beaumont's relationship with his pseudonym, George Stark, and King's relationship with Richard Bachman. Beaumont's motive for creating George Stark differs from King's for creating Bachman. Thad's Stark books make more money than those published under his own name. Thad is the one who has the brain tumor, but it is Stark who dies when his connection to Thad is about to be revealed. It is interesting to watch King use incidents from his life in a work of fiction which, while not mirroring his life, reflects some of his concerns about the relationship between author and work.

## PLOT DEVELOPMENT AND NARRATIVE STRUCTURE

The "Author's Note" that opens *The Dark Half* gives the reader an important clue to the events to come. "I'm indebted to the late Richard Bachman for his help and inspiration. This novel could not have been written without him" (i). The knowledgeable reader immediately recognizes "Richard Bachman" as the pen name used by King for a series of violent novels. The first page of the Prologue is a quotation from *Machine's Way* by Thad's pen name, George Stark. "Cut him," Machine said. "Cut him while I stand here and watch. I want to see the blood flow. Don't make me tell you twice" (1). This quotation from Thad's alter ego, Stark, has a double meaning. It is both an example of the violence which will characterize Stark's appearance and a foreshadowing of the strange surgical procedure detailed in the Prologue.

The Prologue presents the two events from Thad's past which shape the rest of his life. Both happen when he is eleven years old, in 1960. He submits a story to *American Teen* magazine and receives a certificate of merit because he is not really a teen yet. This recognition confirms his desire to become a writer. He also begins to suffer severe headaches, which are accompanied by the sounds of thousands of small birds, sounds so strong he can almost see the birds. Dr. Pritchard diagnoses a brain tumor, which must be removed. When a nurse sees what the surgery reveals, she runs from the operating room. An eye sticks out from the dura, the outer membrane of the brain. The pulsing of the brain makes it look like it is winking. They also find "part of a nostril, three fingernails, and two teeth. One of the teeth had a small cavity in it" (9). These grotesque items are the remnants of a twin absorbed by the stronger fetus. According to Dr. Pritchard, this event is not rare, although he doesn't understand why it happened. The alert reader immediately recognizes this surgery as important, especially when the doctor explains, "Something set this mass of tissue, which was probably submicroscopic in size a year ago, going again. The growth clock of the absorbed twin . . . somehow got wound up again" (10–11). The reader knows that nothing this strange happens just by chance. The doctor may not know what caused it, but we recognize it as the first evidence of forces outside of the natural world at work.

The body of the novel opens with a quotation from another George Stark novel, *Riding to Babylon,* which details another gruesome attack by Alexis Machine, Stark's central character. The description of Machine piercing the eyeball of his victim is quite graphic, but it is important. We immediately make the connection to the eye in Thad's surgery. Machine's last statement to his victim is even more frightening: "I'm back from the dead and you don't seem glad to see me at all, you ungrateful son of a bitch" (13). The return of Machine becomes a clue when King introduces the adult Thad and his wife through a *People* magazine article about them, which opens with a picture of Thad and Liz posing in front of the fake grave of George Stark, 1975–1988. We also learn that Thad and Liz are the parents of young twins, William and Wendy.

When a grave digger finds a strange hole at the exact place where the picture of Thad and Liz was taken, the reader understands what is happening long before any of the characters. The grave digger can't understand why it looks as though someone has dug the hole to escape from a grave. The Sheriff begins the investigation of a violent murder near the cemetery, but we already have a good idea of the killer's identity. We figure out that George Stark refuses to be buried and has come to life.

We know who, but we don't know why. We are willing to believe that Thad's other identity can come to life because we expect unnatural occurrences in a horror novel. We are able to put pieces of evidence together quickly because we have the multiple points of view of the novel available to us. King usually presents the thoughts of the central characters, moving from their viewpoints to his own role as the narrator, the storyteller who remains objective, outside of the action. We connect the information we get from all of these perspectives to understand the plot. In *The Dark Half* we also read pieces of Stark's novel, which give us additional information.

The King fan will recognize the introduction of Sheriff Pangborn, who takes on the traditional investigation of the crimes. His town, Castle Rock, is a King creation used in several novels. When the narrator reminds us of the death of the previous Sheriff by a rabid dog, we know he is talking about *Cujo*. The Sheriff begins his investigation of the death of Homer Gamache by relying on the usual techniques employed by the police. One of his deputies finds a witness who saw a strange man near the sight of the murder. We pick out a detail which doesn't seem important to the police. The witness thinks this man may have come from the direction of Homeland Cemetery.

We may think we understand exactly what is going on, but King throws us off guard by introducing details we do not understand. Dodie Eberhart, a landlady, discovers the body of her boarder, Frederick Clawson, with five words written in blood above his name: "THE SPARROWS ARE FLYING AGAIN" (78). It was Frederick Clawson who discovered George Stark's real identity as Thaddeus Beaumont. His threat to reveal his knowledge prompts Thad to do the *People* magazine article which results in Stark's staged burial. King readers may recognize the author's dark humor in killing Clawson, whose actions parallel those of whoever revealed the connection between Richard Bachman and Stephen King. King tantalizes the reader with connections to the real world which lead us further into his imaginary world.

Stark continues to kill people who had anything to do with helping Thad eliminate him. The police follow Thad, whom they see as their major suspect. Thad knows he must deal with Stark on his own. Thad encounters Rawlie DeLesseps, a fellow professor who teaches a folk myth seminar, and asks him if sparrows have any meaning in American folklore or myth. In Barringer's *Folklore of America* Rawlie learns that "sparrows, loons, and especially whippoorwills are psychopomps" (314). He explains that a "psychopomp" is one who conducts souls between life and death. Rawlie also finds a more ominous association with gatherings of sparrows. These birds have the job of guiding lost souls back into the land of the living. "They are, in other words, the harbingers of the living dead" (314). This information, based in folklore, is the final clue to both understanding and conquering the horror that threatens the hero.

From the moment of this discovery the novel accelerates to the final confrontation between Stark and Thad in Thad's house, where Stark is holding Liz and the twins. The Sheriff attempts to surprise Stark, but he, too, is captured. Thad, armed with his magic wands—the Berol Black Beauty pencils he has always used when writing as Stark—passes through masses of sparrows to his house and his dark half. Stark lets the Sheriff and Liz wait outside while he locks himself, Thad, and the twins in Thad's study. The two men begin to write the novel *Steel Machine.* Thad feels both the tension of the situation and the joy of the act of writing. Over the protests of the part of him that wants to write this book, he lets Stark take over.

When Thad reads what Stark has written he realizes that Stark is not aware that he has been writing the word "sparrow" over and over in the text. While the writing has begun to restore Stark's body, which has been disintegrating throughout the novel, he still does not share Thad's consciousness; he does not know about the sparrows. Finally Thad realizes that he can let go of the book and Alexis Machine. As Stark writes, Thad puts a bird whistle up to his lips and first writes "PSYCHOPOMPS" and then "THE SPARROWS ARE FLYING" (448). The noise of the birds increases as they fly. The sparrows finally break through the wall of the house and carry Stark off. The reader understands Thad's plan, which is the final revelation of the horror novel, the method for eliminating the evil.

The Epilogue begins with a quotation from *The Sudden Dancers* by Thaddeus Beaumont. George Stark is really gone. Thad wants to destroy all evidence of what has happened. The Sheriff has no objection. The evidence of Stark's presence cannot operate according to the laws of detection. As the Sheriff says, "Would anyone believe what it's evidence *of?*" (463). Of course the Sheriff does believe, and he is aware that this may only seem like the end. He wonders if another monster may emerge from Thad's mind sometime in the future. Together they set fire to the house and Stark's car. Sheriff Pangborn hopes that the ashes will be carried to the ends of the earth. Thad stands with his hands over his face.

## CHARACTERS

*The Dark Half* concentrates on only a few characters. Unlike novels where a small group of people work together to fight evil, here only two characters really know what is going on. The central conflict in the novel is based on the relationship between Stark and Thad. Liz and the Sheriff can work only with their limited knowledge.

### Thaddeus Beaumont

The novel opens while Thad is still a child. We learn a little about his supportive mother, Shayla. Thad's father is characterized by his response to the doctor's diagnosis of Thad's tumor; he wants to know how much the operation will cost. We meet Thad through his actions, as he enters the writing contest. We are shocked by the physical contents of his brain before we learn very much about him as a person. The next information about him comes from another outside source, the *People* article. Usually we meet a character slowly and put together clues about personality, history, and profession. King uses these outside sources to present an immediate impression of Thad. If we are to believe in Thad and support him in the face of the evidence against him, we need to know him quickly. We must think Thad is reliable if we are going to trust what he figures out about Stark. But some of what we know about him makes us wonder about him.

In addition to what we learn from other sources, we also see Thad interact with his wife and children. He is uncoordinated physically, but seems to be a loving father and a nice person. We also find out about his relationship with George Stark through the *People* article. This information is followed by Thad's nightmare, in which Stark, driving a black Toronado, takes Thad to his country house on Castle Lake. Stark tells him that the previous owner of the house killed his wife and children and himself. Everything Thad touches in the house crumbles and disintegrates, including the body of Liz. The dream is a warning from Stark. We read about the warning, but we also begin to wonder about the relationship between author and creation. We have no reason to suppose Stark actually exists. Instead we wonder about Thad.

One way the novel operates on us is to cause us to be slightly uneasy about Thad in the beginning. We have to put together all of the different pieces of information and form an opinion about him. We are always measuring Thad against other people's opinions of him, the evidence against him, and what we learn about Stark. When Stark comes alive, Thad must develop as a character in order to deal with him. Thad does not become Stark, but to defeat him he has to learn to think like him. King always uses Thad's first name and Stark's last name. We feel more comfortable with Thad, but we also appreciate his ability to become stronger, to become a heroic man of action in the face of Stark's threat to his family.

However, King lets us know that such changes are not always positive. Thad's return to writing as Stark is dangerous because he is tempted to revive Stark's career. In some ways Stark is part of Thad's character. Thad has created him. At the end of the novel Sheriff Pangborn expresses thoughts we may share. He realizes that one monster has come out of Thad's mind. Stark may be dead, but other monsters might also appear. He thinks that Thad, as Stark's twin, is in some way responsible for what has happened. King never explains clearly how Stark has been created. These concerns about the impact the creator has on his creation must also be important to Thad's creator, Stephen King.

## George Stark

Stark is a strange character. He is the creation of a writer, Thad, who is also the creation of a writer, King. And he is an author who lives out his own work, becoming his creation, Alex Machine. Although we don't know what is happening at the time, the first clue to his change is Thad's dream. Stark drives the car associated with Alex rather than the pickup Thad had given him. We learn about him from the *People* article, but we assume we are dealing with a fictional character who no longer exists. Our first suspicion that he has come to life is the discovery of the open grave.

The inscription on Stark's grave, "Not a Very Nice Guy" (22), echoes King's description of Richard Bachman. Liz suggested that Thad use a pseudonym to free himself from his writer's block. Thad did feel liberated by the use of the pseudonym. He also found it necessary to write in pencil when he was writing as Stark. Using this other name made him feel like he was reinventing himself; the real Thad would be invisible (24). We also learn that the name was suggested by another author's pseudonym. Thad explains that Donald E. Westlake wrote a series under the name Richard Stark. Westlake's alter ego wrote on sunny days, so he had Stark write on rainy ones (24). Stark's background is entirely literary.

We learn about Stark through his words, his thoughts, his actions, and his writing. From all of these sources we get the same message: George Stark is an athletic, agile, violent man who will stop at nothing to achieve his goals. In many ways he is the opposite of Thad. But there is also the suggestion that a part of Stark takes over when Thad writes for him. Once he comes to life apart from Thad, Stark cannot write by himself. He is a powerful creature who cannot really maintain his identity. He literally starts to fall apart during the novel. Thad knows more about Stark than Stark knows about Thad. Stark is not aware of the sparrows. He does not know that he has written about them at murder sites, and he is not aware of them at the end of the book until they break into Thad's study and carry him away. We never doubt Thad's ability to create another voice and call it Stark. What is magic is the idea of Stark actually coming to life. We know that Thad can kill Stark by refusing to write in his voice. But with Stark, King suggests that sometimes an author's creation can get out of control.

## Elizabeth Stephens Beaumont and Wendy and William

As King has developed as an author, he has gradually learned how to create more complete female characters. From the first time we meet Liz, we can believe she is a real woman. The *People* article demonstrates her active role in Thad's career. Their marriage is a partnership. They not only talk to each other, they actually seem to listen to each other. Her belief in Thad confirms his innocence. When Stark captures her, she does not fall apart. She watches for opportunities to attack him. She never gives up, even with her arms and legs taped. At the end, when the sparrows begin to fly, the Sheriff holds her to keep her from dying when she tries to get to the twins and Stark.

Liz is closely connected to the twins. Most of her actions in the novel relate to the family. While the twins are only babies, they are more than just children used as hostages to get Thad to cooperate with Stark. They don't like strangers but are happy and relaxed with Stark. We might expect innocent children to have a heightened awareness of evil, especially in a novel by King. Their reaction to Stark is another indication of his connection to Thad. They sense he is part of their father. The twins also serve as the confirmation of another aspect of Thad's relationship with Stark. Since the twins are of different sexes, they are not identical, but they usually react the same way and have bonds which seem almost supernatural. Their relationship is the pattern for the connection between Thad and Stark.

## Sheriff Alan Pangborn

The Sheriff is part of the world of Castle Rock, the fictional town in Maine used as the setting for several of King's novels. While the Sheriff is an important character in this novel, he is central to *Needful Things*, where all the action takes place in Castle Rock. The town is also featured in *Cujo* and in the Castle Rock Trilogy of "The Sun Dog" from *Four Past Midnight, The Dark Half*, and *Needful Things.* King always has an ambiguous relationship with authority figures, but several of his Maine policemen are good, efficient law enforcers. Their problem is that they are too rational to believe in the irrational horror which can appear so easily in King's world. The Sheriff confronts Thad with clear evidence of his guilt in the murder of Homer Gamache, Stark's first victim. Thad's bloody fingerprints are all over Homer's abandoned truck. But Thad is able to counter with an alibi, a party at his house. Not until the end of the novel can the Sheriff actually believe that Stark is a separate being who was responsible for the murders.

The Sheriff's main role in *The Dark Half* is to investigate crime, especially the murder committed in his territory. But he becomes more involved with the Beaumonts as the novel develops. Once he believes in Thad's story he forms a friendly relationship with the family. He is the only outsider to be a part of the final confrontation between Thad and Stark. He knows he only has a small part, but remembers the old adage that there are no small parts, only small actors (432). At this point in the novel his skills allow him to observe the real connection between Thad and his creation. He realizes that Stark can't see the sparrows. He knows that Thad will have to unmake his own creation and senses how difficult this destruction will be for Thad. He is also a witness to Stark's end, when the sparrows finally carry him away. He sees for himself and he also sees for us, helping us believe what has happened.

## THEME

There are two important themes in *The Dark Half*: the relationship between the creative artist and his work and the idea of the double. While many of King's works explore the importance of the artist, in *The Dark Half* he links this theme to the double, one of the central concerns of horror fiction. Both themes focus on the individual rather than the group. When King concentrates on the individual his themes generally deal with how a person handles problems which challenge moral and ethical codes of conduct. A single person's problems may be confined to the immediate family rather than posing threats to all of society.

In his early fiction King generally relates creativity to the imagination we have as children. As we become adults we lose our sense of wonder, our ability to believe in the reality of the creatures of our imagination. In some novels this loss can be fatal. If we don't believe in monsters we cannot defend ourselves against them. In *The Dark Half* Thad, an author, gives life to imaginary creations. We often judge the success of an author by the believability of her or his characters. Stark is a character who takes on a life of his own, a metaphor for the creative process. King takes this idea literally, but he also takes it one step further. Stark becomes a monster, taking on the identity of his creation, Alex Machine. In King's fiction adults can conquer evil because they retain the imagination of childhood and at the same time distinguish between the real and the imaginary. Adults can believe in monsters, but they also know the difference between monsters in the house and monsters on the page of a book.

When Stark comes alive he is both himself and his creation, Alex Machine. But Stark has no imagination; he cannot see the sparrows. He has no real childhood because he is Thad's creation, existing only because of the strength of Thad's imagination. His physical disintegration during the novel is a reflection of his growing distance from his creator. Stark cannot write; he can only destroy. Stark refuses to die when Thad tries to bury him. King suggests that Thad may not really want him to die; Thad gets pleasure from writing as Stark even though he is not proud of Stark's novels. When Stark acts out the fictional murders Thad has created, Thad must face the consequences of writing such violent fiction. Thad must take responsibility for creating Stark. Through this relationship King examines the concerns any author may have for a creation.

In much of his fiction King is fascinated with the artist. But *The Dark Half* is his most complex examination of the difficulty of writing and the responsibility of the author toward public and creation. Thad is a successful National Book Award nominee who has written two novels under his own name. But he has difficulty writing. He cannot be disturbed, and he writes very slowly. As George Stark he has easily and quickly written four books. Thad's responsible, serious fiction does not sell well. Stark writes violent, amoral thrillers; the first was a best seller, and the others make money. Thad enjoys the money generated by Stark's fiction. He also enjoys the freedom of writing as Stark. Until Stark comes alive he does not understand that he is also responsible for what Stark writes. Thad may have the imagination to believe in monsters, but he has to learn that monsters may be created in our own imaginations.

While Thad says that Stark is not very nice, Alexis Machine is a killer who seems to operate with no controls, no morality. If Stark is Thad's evil twin, he creates and becomes a monster, Machine. As a monster Stark is also like an evil child. He is the child who has never learned to control his desires, the child who will never grow up. He wants immediate gratification. Although we cannot stay children, King wants us to keep the best of childhood. Artists must maintain their connections to childhood. But we must also be able to grow up. If society is to continue we have to become responsible adults.

Thad's relationship to Stark is complicated by his childhood operation—the removal of remnants of a dead twin. The body parts the doctor cuts out of Thad's brain recall the dismembering of Stark's victims, and the pulsing eye which scares the nurse is closely associated with the eyeball Machine pierces. Thad can read Stark's mind the way twins can communicate without words. The Sheriff sees Stark as both more and less than the ghost of Thad's dead twin. And Stark tells the Sheriff and Liz that he comes from a long history of twins (413). Liz had a miscarriage of twins before she had Wendy and William. While authors have to get into the minds of their characters, they must also be able to separate themselves from their creations. Thad must admit his attraction to Stark before he can really destroy him. By introducing the idea of twins, King ties Thad even more closely to Stark than is usual between author and character.

The idea of the double is more general than that of the twin. Some authors explore the idea that every person has a double. Most of us have had the experience of being mistaken for someone else. Authors make these doubles real. In horror fiction the double can be evil, as in the relationship between Thad and Stark. As in *The Dark Half*, the evil double can commit terrible actions, and the good double gets blamed for them.

We can all relate to this situation because we have all been blamed for something we did not do. King pushes this idea into the realm of the supernatural. Thad's double actually exists and commits horrible crimes.

Authors also examine the concept of an internal double. Horror writers are concerned with the evil inside a person, which can express itself as a double. Among the most famous doubles in literature are Dr. Jekyll and Mr. Hyde, who are really two sides of the same person. Authors use this image to deal with the way good people can suddenly do bad things. In *The Cycle of the Werewolf* King explores a good man with a horrible secret self. The werewolf is another traditional version of the horror from within. Many modern horror stories also deal with the way the monster can come from inside a person. Some of the problems faced by our society, such as drug and alcohol abuse, can make people act like monsters, and horror writers are interested in how real these monsters can become.

Sometimes a monster who comes from within can be even more frightening because we may wonder if we too have monsters inside us. When we commit an irrational act or do something bad without thinking, we wonder how we could have done such a thing. *The Dark Half* is an examination of this concept. At the end of *The Dark Half* the Sheriff raises another question when he wonders if there are more monsters inside Thad. Just because we have destroyed a monster who lives in us does not mean there are no others. King wants us to see that possibility. The title of the novel applies to Thad and Stark, but we may all have dark halves waiting to emerge.

Thad has the moral strength to destroy his dark half. The final struggle occurs in the room where Thad writes. The author must come to terms with his creation. He must also deal with the temptations presented by Stark—not just the money, but also the ease of creation. When Thad destroys Stark he accepts a return to the struggle of writing. While Thad must confront his dark half, he is not alone. His twins are also in the room. They represent the innocent world of childhood. They like Stark even though he uses them as hostages. Thad destroys Stark not just for himself. He knows the twins will survive only if they do not have to face two fathers. They are too young to act on their own, and they do not understand evil. They see Stark as a version of their father. The twins have not yet reached the stage in their development where they can imagine that monsters exist. Thad must save himself and them.

We don't know if other monsters exist inside Thad. King does not tell us if Thad has finally removed his evil twin. Thad was unconscious during the first operation to remove his twin. He acts on his own to destroy his double the second time he appears. William and Wendy represent a hope for a future. They are not identical twins, but there is a strong connection between them. This time the connection is good. They help Thad conquer his dark half. Thad makes the right choice, but he must still accept responsibility for creating Stark. No one emerges from a struggle with evil unmarked. We know Thad is the good half, but we may join the Sheriff in wondering how good can create evil. King shows us how doubles can represent the good and evil within us. But he leaves open the question of the source of evil—how and why a dark half appears.

## ALTERNATE READING: HORROR AND MYSTERY GENRES

*The Dark Half* combines two genres to shape the story—horror and mystery. In both mystery and horror, plot is the most important element. The author uses the plot to control the reader's information. The mystery usually begins with a crime. The author provides the reader with clues, some kind of investigator, and, at the conclusion, the solution to the mystery. The horror novel may begin with strange events. At first the characters may try to find natural causes for these events. Gradually they come to believe that there may be supernatural reasons for the occurrences. Characters may find traditional causes for the horror, such as vampires or werewolves. The horror may threaten individuals or society as a whole. By the end of the novel the horror is contained, but it may not be totally destroyed.

Even though the horror at the beginning of *The Dark Half* has a realistic explanation, we recognize that it may be part of a larger pattern. We expect a Stephen King novel to follow the structure of the horror genre. In the horror novel we are gradually introduced to events which have no rational explanation. We are given possible reasons for these events. But we soon find out that conventional reality cannot provide answers to the questions these events raise. The author finally shows us that the source of the horror comes from a world beyond our experience—the world of the supernatural. We often know more than the characters do because we watch everything happen. In *The Dark Half* we know about Homer Gamache's death; we learn about the strange hole in the grass at the cemetery, which suggests someone leaving a grave; we follow Stark and Thad. The author uses our knowledge to gradually lead us to a belief in events that cannot logically happen.

When a horror novel also contains elements of the detective genre, we enjoy watching the events unfold from our privileged position of superior knowledge. In the detective genre the author gives the readers clues and expects them to use these clues to solve the crime. Because detective fiction generally plays fair with readers, we expect to be given all the clues needed to find the murderer. This expectation can also lull us into a false sense of security. We think we are in control of the information; we understand everything that puzzles the characters. At the beginning of *The Dark Half* we think we are supposed to be able to solve the crime. But King does not let us hold this position too long. He introduces Sheriff Pangborn. We recognize him as the typical detective, and we expect to watch him collect the clues we can use to solve the crime. But we have more knowledge than the Sheriff since we can also follow Thad's thoughts. We wonder how two men, Thad and Stark, can have the same fingerprints. We know both Thad and Stark, but we don't really understand how Stark can be alive. Like the Sheriff, we want natural explanations, but we get only supernatural ones.

King maintains the illusion of a continuing dual investigation for much of the novel through the Sheriff, who attempts to retain his rational approach to solving the crime. But his actions become less and less important as more of the conventions of the horror novel take over the plot. The Sheriff finds out about Thad's childhood surgery, but we already know about this and Thad's relationship to Stark. The Sheriff's investigation finally serves to lead him to the point where he will be able to accept a supernatural explanation.

Thad takes control of the novel and his life. Like other heroes of the horror genre, he knows the importance of rational thought. He uses his direct observation of the actions of his twins as clues to his relationship with Stark. But he also trusts to such devices as automatic writing to connect with the mind of his dark half. Once he realizes that Stark is not aware of words about sparrows which appear at crime scenes and in Thad's own writing, Thad also seeks more information about these birds. In the traditional manner of the horror hero, he consults an expert. We are with him when his colleague tells him they are psychopomps who guide lost souls back into the land of the living (314). When he operates as the detective, Thad moves ahead of the reader in finding a solution to the crime because he figures out how to use this knowledge to destroy Stark. He decides he must get Stark writing and then call the sparrows.

We cannot come to the same understanding. The horror novel can contain information which is hidden from the reader for a time. During those moments when Thad works like a traditional detective, he leads the reader to an understanding of a different kind of knowledge—a belief in the supernatural.

Thad, as an artist, doesn't have to make the same shift in beliefs as the Sheriff. He must find the key to understanding the strange events, but he is not limited to understanding them in terms of the rational world. Readers know that Thad is the one to follow because this novel is really a horror story. Our interest in the Sheriff is much like that with which we follow the TV detective Columbo. We want to know how and when he will understand what is really happening, what we already know. The suspense is generated by our hope that he will be in time to help Thad and by our inability to step in and control the process.

King clearly indicates that Thad will not use traditional means of detection. When the Sheriff confronts him with the fingerprints, Thad jokes about the possibility of an identical twin who takes his place while he commits the crimes. The story, which seems crazy to those who listen to it, is amusing for the reader, who is quite certain a kind of twin is committing the crimes. Thad continues by disowning such a classic solution to the mystery: "Well, Stark messed with some of the conventions of the mystery story. Never anything so Agatha Christie as the scenario I just suggested, but that doesn't mean I can't think that way if I put my mind to it" (105). Thad can use reason, but he can also admit the possibility of events beyond reason. The reader too senses that the clue to understanding the story lies in a combining of the two genres. In the traditional mystery the detective reconstructs the crime in order to solve it. Stark's actions have all been directed toward forcing Thad to write another Alexis Machine novel. Thad realizes that he must reconstruct his creation of Stark in order to defeat him.

Mystery and horror fiction end with the destruction of the evil which has threatened the stability of the fictional world. But the closing of a crime novel brings a greater sense of security because murder is an abnormality in rational society. Reason and order are restored through the application of scientific methods or natural human thought processes. The wound may leave a scar, but it closes and heals. The reader at the end of a mystery may be reassured. The crime may be personal, but it has not really touched the reader's life. In the horror novel only the appearance of order is restored. The world of the supernatural is not subject to rational or natural laws. The monster may be destroyed, but the irrational world that created him remains. In the horror novel the evil has been contained, but as readers we are left with a dilemma. If we believe that the events in the novel could happen, we must accept the possibility of the explosion of the irrational. Such a break may be contained, but because it is irrational, it remains a threat. Horror can reappear at any moment in our own lives.

# 7

# *The Dark Tower III: The Waste Lands* (1991)

*The Gunslinger* (1984), *The Drawing of the Three* (1987), and *The Waste Lands* (1991) are the beginning of *The Dark Tower* series, dealing with the journey of Roland of Gilead to the Dark Tower. In this series King combines several genres as he gathers together a group of characters who join Roland in his quest. The overall pattern of the series is shaped by Roland's need to find the dark tower at the center of his world. His journey is like that of the heroes in the fantasy genre who also embark on quests. But the individual novels in the series may actually more closely represent other genres. While the series is set in a post-apocalyptic future, after some great disaster has destroyed much of the world's technology, the cultures King creates seem to return to the images and values of earlier times. The novels depict events we might associate with early American history or even the world of the Middle Ages. The novels move back and forth between our world and this later one. People live with remnants of a former higher level of technology. Everything is decaying; mutants are everywhere. King does not explain what has happened to create this society.

The first novel, *The Gunslinger*, is a compilation of five stories King wrote over a period of twelve years and originally published separately. As the title suggests, this novel contains important elements of the western genre in its characters, setting, and plot. Most of the action takes place in deserts, towns, and outposts. Even though the novel is set in the future, civilization has returned to a simpler time represented by the world of the western. Roland's early training as a gunslinger resembles the training of knights. But he takes on the role of the solitary gunfighter who acts according to a personal code of honor. Roland does what he has been trained to see as right even if it entails violence and killing. He follows a dark man, Walter, through various landscapes. When he finally catches him, Roland realizes that the dark man is a sorcerer. We learn of connections between our world and Roland's world. Jake Chambers, a boy who was pushed into the path of a car on a street corner in Manhattan, appears in Roland's world at a way station, not clear about his transition to Roland's world. Roland, forced to make a choice between his quest for the Dark Tower and the boy, abandons Jake.

The second novel continues the story seven hours after the first one ends. The title, *The Drawing of the Three*, refers to three doors Roland sees on a beach and the people he finds behind those doors. Eddie Dean, who is behind the first door, is a drug addict and a drug runner. Roland brings him into his world. Gradually Eddie accommodates himself to this new world when he falls in love with Odetta, the woman they find behind the second door. Odetta Holmes/Detta Walker, an African American woman, is confined to a wheelchair, having lost her legs in a subway accident. Two different personalities are at war in her body: Odetta is a wealthy civil rights activist, while Detta is a poor woman who sees white males as her oppressors and hates them. Once Detta enters Roland's world through the second door she tries to kill him and Eddie. Jack Mort, who is behind the third door, is a serial killer. He either pushes his victims to their deaths or drops things on them to kill them. Odetta/Detta has been his victim twice. When she was a child he hit her with a brick, which sent her into a coma and created the personality of Detta. Later he pushed the adult Odetta into the path of a subway train. Roland also begins to suspect Jack Mort of pushing Jake Chambers in front of a car and causing his death. The time connections between the two worlds are so complex that Roland does not know if Jake is still alive and if he can still save him. As King points out in *The Waste Lands*, if Jake is still alive, how can Roland remember him (3–4)? Odetta/Detta becomes a new personality, Susannah Dean. Her first name is the middle name of her two previous personalities, and her last name acknowledges her symbolic marriage to Eddie. At the end of the novel the same subway train which took Susannah's legs kills Jack Mort sixteen years later.

The third novel, *The Waste Lands*, picks up the characters and adventures several months after the end of *The Drawing of the Three* and ends with the characters still on their journey. The Afterword to *The Drawing of the Three* suggests that there may eventually be a total of six or seven books in the series. The fourth volume, *Wizard and Glass*, which has yet to appear, will cover events in Roland's past in the period before the first novel. King admits that he does not know how the story will end or even if Roland will ever reach the tower (400). The novels should be read in order because each refers to events in previous volumes. Once introduced, characters continue to appear in succeeding books. The illustrations which accompany the texts give us another view of this strange world. All of the novels in this series have difficult places where everything is not as clear or as fully explained as we might expect in King's fiction. *The Dark Tower* has influenced both *Insomnia* and *Rose Madder* and may affect the further development of all of King's fiction.

## PLOT DEVELOPMENT AND NARRATIVE STRUCTURE

The characters have moved inland from the beach at the opening of *The Waste Lands*. The novel is divided into two books, titled "Jake" and "Lud." Each book is further divided into titled chapters with further subdivisions. King numbers the chapters consecutively from book to book, the way he usually organizes his fiction. Three epigraphs set the tone for the novel. The first, from T. S. Eliot's poem "The Waste Land," provides subtitles for Book One ("fear in a handful of dust") and Book Two ("A heap of broken images"). The reference to Eliot's poem and its bleak hopelessness sets the tone for the novel. The second epigraph links King's Roland with Childe Roland of Robert Browning's poem "Childe Roland to the Dark Tower Came." The final quotation, from "Hand in Glove" by Robert Aickman, also refers to waste. This time it is the name of a river.

Even though King begins in the middle of a longer story, the novel has its own organization. *The Waste Lands* follows the adventures of the central characters as they continue their journey to the Dark Tower. But the story also tracks Jake in our world as he moves toward his reunion with Roland. The reunited characters then follow various clues to the next stage of their quest.

The opening sentences show characters learning to shoot like gunslingers. King gives small hints about each character, allowing us to follow the action if we have not read the other volumes in the series. Roland is teaching Susannah and Eddie to shoot. Throughout the novel King involves us in one action and then introduces a second source of tension as one way to keep us involved. He gives us only a little information at a time, moving back and forth from action to information about each character. As the narrator moves among the minds of the characters, we get a more complete idea of what is happening than we would by observing events from the viewpoint of a single character.

To Eddie's life with Henry, his dead brother in our world, King opposes Eddie's life in this new world. Eddie begins to realize the false picture he has of his past. King maintains narrative tension during these memories because we are aware that a seventy-foot bear with something strange on its head is racing toward Eddie full of hatred for humans. Susannah must test her new shooting skills to destroy the bear and save Eddie. She is concerned about the feeling she has when she actually shoots to kill. She feels cold, but she also cannot wait to do the same thing again. She now understands something more about Roland and what it is to be a gunslinger. He explains that the bear is a Guardian created by the Great Old Ones, and that it is two or three thousand years old. The Great Old Ones made twelve Guardians to guard the twelve portals in and out of their world. The cook in his father's castle told Roland that these portals were the last creation of these people. If we think of the portals forming a circle, a line drawn from each to the center would mark the location of the Dark Tower.

The group realizes that they can retrace the trail of Shardik, the robot bear, and move straight forward from the portal to the Dark Tower. Roland finally has a plan, but at the same time he feels that he is losing his sanity. He is bewildered by a puzzle he cannot solve. He is haunted by the story of Jake. His mind cannot deal with the idea of multiple time lines existing together. If Jake is not yet dead, there is no way he could have met him and abandoned him to another death. Jake should have lived sometime between the New York of Eddie in 1987 and the New York of Susannah in 1963. Roland tries to relive his experiences to see if he really did meet Jake. The characters receive images which connect them with each other. Eddie dreams of the places Jake will encounter when King returns to the boy's adventures. Eddie sees a magic shop called the House of Cards, and Tom and Gerry's Artistic Deli in his sleep. When he dreams that he turns the key in the lock of the deli, the door opens on a vision of the Dark Tower.

As the group follows the bear's path, they come across evidence that this world is slowly running down. They also discover connections to

Jake's world. Eddie remembers a childhood experience with a wreck of a house in New York known as the Mansion. Like the Marsten House in *'Salem's Lot*, it has the reputation of being haunted. At the portal the group finds where one of the Beams which hold the world together begins. The Beam should lead to the Tower, but the distance along the Beam is growing longer because this world is slowing down, and its space is expanding.

The next chapter returns us to a familiar time and place as we observe Jake's growing madness because he feels the pull of Roland's world. We learn about Jake and his father. His relationship with his father is similar to that of fathers and sons in many of King's novels. In order to survive, the boy has to find a substitute for the father, who does not understand him or his situation. He hears voices discussing his death while he is at school. Pieces of his meeting with Roland float through his mind. An essay he has written, which expresses some of these feelings and is almost like unconscious or automatic writing, gets a good grade because the teacher thinks it is original. It deals with Roland and seems to contain hints about the future. We also recognize the quotation "fear in a handful of dust" and another quotation from Robert Browning. Jake gives the poets Eliot and Browning the nicknames "Butch" and "Sundance" (97), suggesting a connection to the gunslinger. While we recognize some of the characters, we wonder about "Blaine" and the riddles which accompany this name. At the end of the essay "Choo-choo" is repeated numerous times, along with Jake's admission that he is afraid. The final page of the essay has a picture of the Leaning Tower of Pisa, which he has colored black. He cannot remember creating any of the essay.

King has Jake think back to the moment when his double life seems to start as a way of including more of his story. It is the day he suddenly sees that he is going to die but does not, the day when, as Roland explained it, he entered the force of his *ka-tet*. We have an even more complex feeling because we have already seen this moment from Roland's perspective. Jake cannot concentrate, so he leaves school. As the day progresses he collects the items he will need for the new journey. He does not really understand why he acts, but does things because he is drawn to them. In a bookstore owned by Calvin Tower he gets *Charlie the Choo-choo* and *Riddle-De-Dum! Brain-Twisters and Puzzles for Everyone!* The answer section is missing from the riddle book. As he walks he is able to anticipate what will happen next, even to hearing a fragment of a Rolling Stones song, the same one Eddie has sung earlier in the novel. King balances the connections between the two worlds with this reference and the next sign Jake finds. He ends up at a construction site where he finds a sign for Tom and Gerry's Artistic Deli, which has already been a part of one of Eddie's dreams. Jake wishes Roland could decide if he is alive or dead. King expects us to constantly make the connections between the two worlds. But, like the characters, we see that pattern pieces are missing, and we still have no idea what will happen next.

We also begin to see the complexities of the dual time which operates in the novel. Rather than alternating, the stories run parallel, with one breaking into the other. In the final chapter of this section the two time lines finally connect. The relationship between the times in the two worlds is complex because two days have passed in Roland's world and three weeks in Jake's. His group reaches the Great Road, which was built many years ago. The two quests become even more entangled. The group moves on and finds a marker that tells them they have come to Mid-World, once a large kingdom. As with time, space is also coming together; the path of the Beam and the Great Road are the same. Both lead to a once great city, Lud, at the end of this kingdom, but Roland is certain it too is in ruins.

Finally the two worlds meet. Jake is attacked as he struggles to pass through a door in the Mansion into Roland's world. Roland jumps through the door and redeems his earlier betrayal of Jake by grabbing him and retreating back through the door. Eddie shuts the door. Roland promises not to drop Jake again, but wonders if he will be able to keep his promise.

King does not want to let us feel any relief that our heroes are out of danger. Stopping points are used to give us information we will need to follow the plot and anticipate problems the group will face. The group finally rests when they come to a town, River Crossing, and become the guests of its few remaining citizens. Aunt Talitha and other residents tell about the city ahead and the people who still live there—two warring groups, the Pubes and the Grays. We also learn about a new character, Blaine the monorail. One monorail once ran into the city. It no longer works, but Blaine may still run out of the city. The group realizes that they must go through the city to get to Blaine, which will take them along a Beam toward the Tower. We know that they will not have an easy trip.

King never lets up the suspense. Even the entry to the city becomes a trial. The bridge they must cross has almost disintegrated. Once they cross they meet Gasher, who threatens them with a grenade unless they give him Jake. While Eddie and Susannah make their way to the train station, Roland rescues Jake. The horrors of life in the city are problems for all of them. Eddie and Susannah must fight a mob, while Roland must avoid many booby traps on his way to free Jake. For both groups the city is another proving ground for their skills. Their difficulties also signal the disintegration of this civilization.

Both groups must solve puzzles once they get to their goals. No door opens easily in this novel. The entry which protects Blaine has a numerical puzzle and a security code. When Eddie and Susannah communicate with Blaine he wants them to ask a riddle or he will kill them. When Tick-Tock Man is introduced we realize we have met him before, as Randall Flagg. This time he calls himself Richard Fannin, but he is clearly the same man in the same old worn boots who set up an evil empire in Las Vegas in *The Stand*. He even repeats Trashcan Man's lines from that novel. He is trying to prevent Roland and his group from reaching the Tower. The reunited group finally solves the puzzle of Blaine's number and gets on board the monorail as the city fills with poisonous gas. But at the end of the novel they are in even more trouble, trapped on Blaine, who intends to kill them. Roland makes a deal with him. If Blaine fails to solve all of their riddles he will take them to Topeka, where they can continue their quest. But if he wins they will die. Blaine is another machine gone insane. We are left with some possibilities for escape but no answers. King is preparing us for the next volume of this story.

## CHARACTERS

The complex plot of *The Waste Lands* leaves little room for character development. King has already introduced the major characters in the earlier books in the series. In this volume we learn more about Roland's world and how Eddie and Susannah adapt to it. These two spend much of their time reacting to situations. Eddie's struggle with his addiction and his conflicts with Roland about being pulled out of New York are already resolved. Susannah's two different personalities are now united. They both gain skills as gunslingers, and their skills are tested when they must kill. They both love and fear their feelings when they act as gunslingers. Eddie and Susannah also discover that they actually prefer Roland's world to their own. They become dedicated to the quest for the Dark Tower. But they also remain somewhat stereotyped characters.

### Susannah

Susannah has many interesting traits, and King places her in situations where she does not react as a stereotypical female. But we still have the sense King is not challenging female stereotypes. The illustrations of Susannah and Eddie in *The Waste Lands* resemble comic book figures. They are versions of action heroes and share their traits. Female action figures are often as violent as their male counterparts. At times we wonder why Susannah has been given a major handicap that limits her mobility. And she is given the typically female role of seducer. Roland tells Susannah she must distract a demon while Eddie opens the door for Jack. It seems that demons can be male or female, and they have a weakness for sex. Roland tells her that they may have to call on Detta's strength if the demon is male. King does not suggest that demons might prefer their own sex, and we are not surprised that the demon who attacks Susannah is a male. In some of his recent books King creates interesting women with nontraditional roles. But Susannah is forced into a sexual relationship, while the men are tested by traditional male forms of combat.

### Eddie

Eddie grows to share the role of male hero with Roland, becoming more of an equal when he starts to use some of his own unique abilities. He revives his interest in carving, a skill that turns out to be crucial. Eddie must carve a key to rescue Jake. He has trouble finishing it in time, and Roland forces him to confront his fears. He is then able to finish the carving and open the door. But Eddie still cannot operate totally on his own. Roland helps him with Jake, and Susannah as Detta solves the numerical puzzle to open Blaine's door. Eddie's relationship with his dead older brother Henry makes him more sensitive to other people, but at the same time more vulnerable. Roland teaches him to control his concern for others and to act more directly. Both he and Susannah learn to shoot with their minds and kill with their hearts. By the end of this novel Eddie has found this balance.

### Jake

We learn more about Jake's background, but he remains an eleven-year-old boy who is just finishing sixth grade. He resembles many other boys in King's fiction. He comes from a family with a verbally abusive father and a mother who is afraid of her husband. He leaves his family and finds a new, more successful one. The only difference in this series is Roland's failure to keep Jake alive the first time they meet. Just as the story dominates the characters, Roland's quest is more important to him than protecting Jake.

### Roland

Roland is the only central character who reveals other sides to his personality. He still refuses to tell the story of his youth because it is not the right time. In *The Drawing of the Three,* he suffered from physical problems. In this novel he is tested mentally by the confusion he feels in attempting to reconcile the dual time lines concerning Jake. He is still the teacher, but his pupils have almost mastered their lessons. They can act successfully on their own. Roland is the person who has the knowledge necessary for the quest, although others add facts as they go along. Even though his flaws are visible, he holds the group together.

## THEME

*The Waste Lands,* like the other volumes in the series, develops four themes: the destruction of our environment, the relationship between father and son, the divisions which separate individuals, and the connection between free will and fate. King's post-apocalyptic fiction, which includes *The Stand* and *The Dark Tower* series, explores a ruined planet and asks how we have come to destroy our world. He examines the parent/child relationship in many of his novels as sons look for substitute fathers. In *The Drawing of the Three* and *The Waste Lands* doors separate characters and worlds. In *The Dark Tower* series King explains a view of interaction between the cycle of life and destiny.

King sees the abuse of our planet leading us to destruction. He uses the future in *The Dark Tower* novels to demonstrate what we are on the way to becoming. The first two novels show a future world with strange creatures. Roland crosses a large desert in *The Gunslinger* and must fight mutants. Much of his journey is new to him. The world of Roland's youth has already been destroyed before this novel begins. We share Roland's sense of loss because the world of his youth is like our age of chivalry, which is also gone. By the time we reach *The Waste Lands* the ruin of the planet is more important than the destruction of Roland's childhood. In this world the remnants of a technologically advanced society are gradually falling apart. A robot attacks Eddie; Lud runs down; Blaine carries the group off. In the countryside some people can still live in peace, but in the city there is only destruction.

In addition to demonstrating what might happen to our world if we don't change, King also stresses certain values, showing moral characters who can survive in any place and demonstrating the traits they need to go on. These traditional virtues are contrasted to the characteristics which caused the destruction and those the bad characters demonstrate. The good characters adapt to this new world, but the evil characters retain the very traits which destroyed the old world.

The comparisons between Roland's world and our own show the danger of abusing our natural resources. King also uses these two worlds to analyze human relationships—especially those between father and son. Roland suffers because he does not know what has happened to Jake. He knows he betrayed the boy when he chose the quest over the boy's life in *The Gunslinger*. But he cannot reconcile the complexities of the time relationships between his world and that of the boy. If Jake was pushed in front of a car before his first appearance in Roland's world, how could he be alive in that world? If Jake died in Roland's world, is he still alive in his own world? Roland has evidence of Jake's presence, but he does not really know if they have met. While King presents Roland's dilemma, he also depicts Jake's family life. Jake's father shows concern only when the boy disturbs his father's schedule. Jake's mother absents herself from conflict with tranquilizers. When Jake finally enters Roland's world the gunslinger must face further tests to assume the role of the boy's father. King's characters often take on the role of surrogate father, but in *The Waste Lands* Roland must prove his worthiness because of his earlier betrayal of Jake's trust.

The two other members of Roland's group must also work through aspects of the parent/child relationship. Eddie has grown up without a father. His older brother acts like a father, but he is a false father figure, guiding Eddie into drug use. Eddie takes care of his brother until he finally understands that he must abandon this destructive relationship. Susannah has had a more positive childhood, but to unite the two halves of her personality she too must leave her past behind. King shows that we have to understand our past, but we must live in the present to achieve anything worthwhile with our lives.

If we are to grow we must cross the boundaries between our past and our present. Doors are symbols of transitions in *The Dark Tower* series, both connecting and dividing. In *The Drawing of the Three* Roland moves back and forth between the two worlds by means of the doors on the beach. In *The Waste Lands* there are several types of doors. To escape the Mansion and enter Roland's world Jake must have a key—a key he almost loses. Eddie must make the key, reproducing one he sees in a vision, and must draw a picture of the door. Eddie's act adds the role of the artist or the creator to Jake's courage. These characteristics must operate together. They must all work as a group for this transfer to take place. Roland must be willing to risk his quest this time to pull Jake through the door. Roland must find the secret to Tick-Tock Man's door to rescue Jake a second time. Jake also works from the inside to locate the right button to open the door. The group works together to solve the puzzle which opens the barrier to Blaine. Roland must help Susannah remember the voice of her father and become Detta to deal with the numbers puzzle. But Jake adds the final clue about the numbers being touched backwards. When they pass through the grilled gate to Blaine, this barrier separates them from the destruction Blaine is letting loose on the city. But they also become trapped by their own deadly pact with Blaine. Blaine locks them in the train as he races along his track toward his destruction. King leaves the characters caught as they try to find a riddle Blaine cannot solve. But by leaving them trapped, he has opened the door to yet another novel in the series.

Doors divide, but they also reveal. What is on both sides of the doors is important if Roland and his group are going to survive. King shows us the boundaries and then shows us how they must be crossed. Many of these doors are tied to technology. King sees technology as a destructive force that, along with such human traits as greed, has brought about the destruction of Roland's world. Only those with good motives can avoid being destroyed by it. King shows various ways we can move between the worlds and within them, but only a few survivors can move through this landscape. King suggests that we should examine ourselves and our relationship with technology and our planet. We must also decide whether we would have the ability to survive in Roland's world.

We need to know if we would have the necessary courage and self-sacrifice. He wants us to know that we must all form our own groups if we are going to make our way through the doors in our own lives.

King also establishes the connections between our world, New York as we know it, and Roland's world, set in some future time. These connections become part of a larger pattern. Roland tries to understand this pattern as destiny, or as he calls it in High Speech (the language of his father's world), "*ka*." He combines this word, which he sees as more complex than destiny, with "*tet*," which is a group of people who share the same interests and goals. The place where lives are joined by fate is "*ka-tet*." *Ka-tet* would have put all the right people in the right place for Jake to have died when Roland intervened. He prevented Jake from being pushed into the street and dying into Roland's world. This act causes confusion because Roland's first encounter with Jake is based on Jake's dying into Roland's world. At the same time Roland remembers Jake's other death, which he caused when he abandoned the boy in *The Gunslinger*. Roland chooses to prevent Jake's death—an act which changes the chain of events. But Roland cannot accept the fact that he has changed the past. The two realities tear Roland apart until he saves Jake from death a second time by pulling the boy into his world. Roland calls the group which has joined the quest to the Dark Tower *ka-tet* as well. All the group members feel a sense of destiny, but they must perform their tasks successfully to fulfill their destiny. King juggles this seeming contradiction throughout *The Dark Tower* series as he tries to work out the relationship between the actions characters take and the role destiny plays in their lives.

## ALTERNATE READING: GENRES

King deliberately works in several genres in *The Dark Tower* series. The first novel, *The Gunslinger*, contains many elements of the western, an unexpected genre for King. The central character is like a western hero, especially those played by Clint Eastwood, such as the Man with No Name. Roland wanders from place to place, generally doing good, but he is also capable of committing violent actions, especially in revenge for evil done to him. For the most part the settings are appropriate for the genre; the action takes place in small western towns, large stretches of desert, and small outposts where riders can change horses. But some details do not fit. Westerns are set in the past in the United States. This novel is set in an unknown country at some point in the future. Roland seems to follow a code of behavior associated with the western hero. He carries two guns, which he uses in self-defense. He is a loner who fights to support civilization. He must look toward the future even though he longs for a more chivalrous past. The gunslinger's training is also associated with that of knights. Roland and his companions are taught their skills in his father's castle. One of the central characters is a sorcerer, and Jake appears from another world.

King is attempting something different in setting out to write a series of novels following Roland's quest for the Dark Tower. He has maintained his interest in this story over a long period of time. Perhaps because he did not set out to write for a large audience in this series he felt a certain freedom to experiment. He uses the elements of a variety of genres as he needs them. We still recognize these elements even though we may be surprised at how he combines them.

In both *The Drawing of the Three* and *The Waste Lands* King moves away from the western genre. Small pieces remain in the gunslinger's title and occupation. But these novels move to the epic fantasy, post-apocalyptic, and science fiction genres King used in *The Stand*. The post-apocalyptic novel presents a world after some great event has occurred. The survivors of the disaster struggle to restore elements of the past or attempt to find new ways to live in this ruined world. The epic novel often uses fantasy and a mythical setting to feature a heroic quest. King does not specifically refer to J. R. R. Tolkien's *The Lord of the Rings*, another series of novels that features a group on a quest. King directly refers to fantasy fiction when he calls the robot bear Shardik, borrowed from *Shardik* by Richard Adams. Fantasy can be set in many periods, but we often associate it with an undefined time which suggests a medieval past and relies on sorcerers and magic spells for many of its effects. Science fiction is set in the future and is associated with realistic stories which examine the effect of technology on society. While it might not seem possible for these seemingly contradictory genres to appear in the same story, King combines them in *The Drawing of the Three* and *The Waste Lands*.

He puts the two genres together especially well in *The Waste Lands*. Characters work with both magic and technology to follow their quest. The novel's opening still has elements of the western as Eddie and Susannah learn to shoot. They are impressed by Roland's ability to draw his gun quickly. Once they set out again on their quest, fantasy and science fiction work together. Much of the history Roland tells the others seems to come from a mythical past. But the bear Shardik and similar creatures are the result of technology. The complex time lines King juggles in this novel aid in blurring the distinctions between the genres. The reality of the scenes in the present makes us believe in a future which connects the novel to the science fiction genre. But the magic Roland, Eddie, and Susannah use to get Jake makes us think of fantasy. We don't usually meet demons in science fiction.

King blends these two genres without making us wonder about their contradictions by moving quickly back and forth between two worlds. We see events from one world appearing in the other world. We learn to expect the unexpected. We accept a rose and a key which appear in a vacant lot in New York. We even accept the horror elements in Jake's experience in the Mansion. The bear might be a monster, but it turns out to be a robot. King provides such a unique experience that we are willing to accept conflicting genres. We follow the characters in worlds which are both like ours and very different. We may not know what will come next, but we are involved in these worlds. The various genres serve as guides to help us move through this series.

# 8

# *Needful Things* (1991)

*Needful Things* is King's last novel to deal with the fictional town of Castle Rock. The town, whose name comes from a Frank Sinatra song of the fifties, is familiar from several earlier works. While King considers *The Dark Half,* "The Sun Dog," and *Needful Things* the Castle Rock trilogy, the town is the setting of novels such as *Cujo, The Dead Zone,* and the short story, "The Body." King explains that he is leaving Castle Rock because it is too familiar. He would rather be less comfortable in his writing. Working with a town whose map he can draw discourages him from taking risks (Beahm, *Stephen King Story* 151). Castle Rock is located near Durham, Maine, where his family moved when he was eleven (Beahm, *Stephen King Story* 19). The Durham of King's youth is the model for Castle Rock (Beahm, *Stephen King Story* 27). The two major divisions of the novel are illustrated with woodcut images, and each chapter begins with a small woodcut. Bill Russell did the illustrations for this text and carries on with this style in *Dolores Claiborne.*

*Needful Things* also brings back an important character from an earlier novel, Sheriff Alan Pangborn of *The Dark Half. Needful Things* features a large number of characters who interact as the story progresses. While he experiments with the horror genre in many of his recent works, King returns to his traditional view of horror in *Needful Things.* Supernatural events dominate the plot. While people act realistically, they are motivated by an evil power. King treats the horror genre seriously in *Needful*

*Things*, but he also portrays the interactions of the citizens of Castle Rock humorously.

## PLOT DEVELOPMENT AND NARRATIVE STRUCTURE

King opens *Needful Things* with a short chapter called "You've Been Here Before." Here he talks to his readers as though they have just returned to Castle Rock. With a folksy tone he sets the time of year—October. As we sit with him on the steps of the bandstand, he introduces the people who pass and tells a little bit about their relationships, focusing on the aggravations between people. This casual information sets up the personal conflicts which will result in the destruction of Castle Rock. We see the signs Wanda Hemphill, a Baptist, has put up protesting the Casino Nite the Catholics are planning at the Knights of Columbus Hall. The religious leaders of the two congregations, Father Brigham and Reverend William "Willie" Rose, have done nothing to stop the friction between the two groups. We learn about some of the women in town. Myrtle Keeton is worried because her husband Dan, the head selectman, is disturbed about something. Leonore Potter, who takes great pride in her flowers, is considered snooty by the rest of the town.

The narrator then brings us up to date on some of the past history of the town, events covered in previous King fiction. He tells us about Frank Dodd of *The Dead Zone*, Joe Camber and Sheriff Bannerman of *Cujo*, and Pop Merrill of "The Sun Dog." He summarizes other conflicts between Henry Beaufort and Hugh Priest, and Wilma Jerzyck and Nettie Cobb. He informs us that Sheriff Alan Pangborn has lost his wife and younger child and that Polly Chalmers is suffering from arthritis. He ends by telling us that all these events will mean nothing compared to the opening of a new store down the street from where Pop Merrill's junk shop, the Emporium Galorium, used to be. The store's name is Needful Things, and it is about to get its first customer.

After this beginning the novel is divided into three parts: Grand Opening Celebration, The Sale of the Century, and Everything Must Go. It ends with another version of "You've Been Here Before." The action covers eight days, from Tuesday, October 8, to Tuesday, October 15. Each day is clearly marked to help us follow the passage of time. The folksy speaker disappears, and the main body of the novel is told in the voice of a third person narrator who can either remain outside of the characters or move from mind to mind sharing their thoughts with the reader. King picks up the story where the folksy narrator left off. The first sentence not only establishes the focus for this section of the novel but also tells a lot about life in Castle Rock. "In a small town, the opening of a new store is big news" (13). King then introduces the first victim of this new store, eleven-year-old Brian Rusk. A sign announces that Needful Things is a new kind of store where you won't believe your eyes (13). King shows how various people in town react to the store mostly through Brian's eyes. When Brian notices that the store is open, he goes in even though his mother has shown more interest in it.

If we are aware of the horror tradition, we know that Brian should be careful. The owner welcomes him with echoes of Count Dracula's famous words, "Come in my friend. Enter freely, and leave some of the happiness you bring" (22). Dracula says almost exactly the same words to Harker except for the substitution: "Come freely. Go safely . . ." (Stoker 20). The owner, Leland Gaunt, claims to be from Akron, Ohio. Brian thinks the jacket he is wearing may actually be a smoking jacket like Sherlock Holmes wears. This first meeting with Gaunt establishes the strange nature of his store and its contents. Brian holds a splinter from Noah's Ark and has an image of actually being on it. We get a better idea of how Gaunt operates when he gets Brian to tell him what he wants most in the world—a '56 Sandy Koufax card. When Gaunt locates the card it is not only the perfect card, it is signed for Brian. Even though Gaunt claims this is just a coincidence, we know these kinds of coincidences don't just happen, especially in horror fiction.

We are concerned when Gaunt negotiates with Brian for the card. The price is just below the amount of money Brian has in his pocket. But there is an additional price. We do not learn exactly what it is, but it involves Wilma Jerzyck, Brian's neighbor. With this transaction King establishes the pattern Gaunt will use to involve the whole town in a network of "deeds" leading to the destruction of Castle Rock. After Brian's purchase King describes the attitude of a small New England town to a new shop. He explores the relationship between curiosity and a conservative code where certain things are just not done. He lists the rules which should be followed: you should not be the first to come or the last to go; you should not show too much interest in the contents of the shop or the background of the owner; and you should not bring a welcome-to-town present such as homemade baked goods. But one resident of the town does not follow its rules.

Polly Chalmers has a history which fascinates the other residents of the town. Her eccentricity is confirmed when people see her bringing a

Tupperware container containing a cake to the new store right after it officially opens. When she meets the owner she has the sense she already knows him even though she is sure she doesn't. She immediately feels the charm of this stranger. But we sense that King wants us to watch Gaunt very carefully. We may even wonder if there is a little irony in the fact that Polly has brought him a devil's food cake. We observe the shop through Polly's eyes. She sees it as a curio shop and notices that there are no price tags on any of the items. We also learn about the terrible arthritis in her hands, which is even more of a problem because she runs a sewing shop. As they discuss the people in the town we find out that Nettie Cobb, who works for Polly, made the cake. Leland explains that he doesn't price anything because he enjoys bargaining or "defining worth by need" (48). Even though Polly really likes him, we are worried. After she leaves the shop his smile, showing "his uneven teeth, . . . became unpleasantly predatory" (48). We are even more concerned when he states that Polly will do.

King continues to detail all of the customers who enter Gaunt's shop, the negotiations, and the purchases. He develops the personality traits of each character and their reactions. Gradually people leave with their "needful thing" and some unstated agreement to play a little trick on someone, to do a little deed. Some customers make a good bargain, and Gaunt waits to trap them into another kind of action. He promises another object to match the one they have. Once they have discovered how much they want the original piece they will agree to anything to get its mate. Near the end of this section Polly finally agrees to try a charm which will cure her arthritis.

The first section of the novel also puts in motion the events Gaunt has established with his sales. It covers the longest period of time, from Tuesday through Sunday. While Gaunt will start a few new feuds between people, he concentrates on controlling people who already have enemies. He has most of the people in town in his power by the end of this section. We also begin to understand the kinds of pranks he asks people to perform and the pattern of destruction he creates. We also become aware that he is some kind of monster. The other person to recognize that he is not human is Brian Rusk, who commits suicide because he cannot deal with this knowledge. Nettie and Wilma meet and kill each other in the first section. Their horrible fight to the death is the signal of what is to come. Gaunt is pleased with what he has accomplished so far. He sees himself as an electrician, cross wiring connections between people. When the wiring is finished he will turn up the voltage all the way. Gaunt does this not just out of malice; he is collecting souls like trophies. But he is also amused by what happens. As he views the town, he also decides to hire an assistant.

The second section of the novel covers a shorter period of time, from Sunday to part of Monday. The last section covers from quarter to six on Monday night through the destruction of the town later that night. Gaunt hires Ace Merrill, who has just returned to town to avoid people he owes $80,000 for a drug deal gone bad. On Monday, which is also Columbus Day, the people of Castle Rock discover unpleasant things about each other. The various lies Gaunt has caused others to plant being to surface. We watch the reactions as each prank is revealed and begin to anticipate what will happen. Some of the events on this Monday don't appear to be that bad. Less likable people seem to bring on their own trouble because they believe what they find and don't actually talk to the other person involved. We can understand that Wilma and Nettie, who were already enemies, might believe the other had done something terrible. But at first we are less sympathetic with people who find forged love letters and believe them.

Gaunt also attacks Alan and Polly in this section. They are lovers and care deeply about each other. Gaunt avoids meeting Alan until the end of the novel. He uses the pasts of these two people to set them against each other. Polly has hidden the cause of her son's death from Alan. Alan still cannot deal with the death of his wife and one son. Alan works to undo the evil Gaunt creates even though he is not aware of the source. He concentrates on the cause of the final confrontation between Nettie and Wilma. The sequence of the events does not work for him, and he begins to suspect that others are involved.

The second section ends with most of the action under way. Gaunt teams up Ace Merrill and Buster Keeton. Buster and Ace set bombs connected to timers all over town. Buster wants to die, and Gaunt convinces him to take his enemies with him. By this point we can see the direction the story is taking. Our main concern is for the positive characters, especially Polly and Alan. King interrupts our observation of Buster and Alan with the more humorous battle between the Catholics and the Baptists over the casino night fund-raiser. The fight is now fueled by Gaunt's intervention. Both sides are attacked by similar bombs at their meetings. King alternates the movements of these two groups with individual acts of destruction.

A state trooper who is investigating the murders in town tries to stop the battle between the two religious groups. Even additional troopers can't halt the fighting. King once again introduces other actions in the middle of this event. Alan returns to town after getting information from Brian's brother. Some people finally realize how Gaunt has manipulated them. Polly rids herself of Gaunt's charm. Meanwhile Ace and Buster are making and setting their bombs. As all of the groups come together, Alan is sidetracked when he believes that a videotape of his wife's death Gaunt has left for him is authentic. King moves everyone into the final confrontations that will end in the destruction of Castle Rock.

As the bombs go off, Polly manages to show Alan how he has been fooled by Gaunt. Alan finally confronts this monster. He uses a magic trick to bring the forces of good to his side. He wants to distract Gaunt by making flowers appear from his watch. The ghosts of previous events in the town appear to Alan during this final showdown. He sees the sparrows from *The Dark Half* and the dogs from *Cujo* and "The Sun Dog." The Sheriff cannot kill Gaunt, but he manages to grab a bag that contains the souls Gaunt has taken from his customers. When Alan pulls the string to release the flowers, he releases a "bouquet of light" (679) which forces Gaunt to retreat. Polly joins Alan in defending the bag of souls. Gaunt finally changes shape and flies away. The violent storm which has been raging suddenly stops. The few survivors take each other to the hospital.

Alan and Polly leave behind a town which no longer exists. The accumulation of events which has plagued Castle Rock for so many years is over. King has one last message for the reader. The final section of *Needful Things* mirrors the opening. The folksy narrator has returned, but he is in another town, Junction City. A new store is about to open. This time it's called Answered Prayers. King is telling us that he, too, will go on in another location. Castle Rock is gone, but he will find new towns for his horror.

## CHARACTERS

Many characters interact in *Needful Things*, but only a few are fully developed. Most of the people in Castle Rock are defined by their needful things and what they are willing to do to get them. Even though we may learn a little about people like Ace Merrill and Buster Keeton, we deal only with the surfaces of these personalities. King deliberately keeps us in the dark about Gaunt, a character who represents absolute evil. Like Barlow in *'Salem's Lot*, he is a supernatural creation who looks human but does not share many human traits. We share his view of the town at certain key moments, but he never really exists as a person. The few characters we get to know in detail change as the novel progresses. Brian Rusk, Alan Pangborn, Polly Chalmers, and, to a lesser extent, Norris Ridgewick have both good and bad characteristics and more fully developed personalities.

## Sheriff Alan Pangborn

King introduces the Sheriff as he returns from Portland, where he has been testifying in several court cases. We first see him defined by his job. Throughout the novel changes in his personality are connected to his investigations. But King also includes details which begin to give us another view of this man. We see him driving a station wagon which he calls the ultimate unmarked car, a family vehicle. He is also depressed. We soon learn the major reason for his depression, the loss of his wife, Annie, and his son, Todd. The car holds memories of family events. For Alan it still contains their ghosts. He finds a trick can in the glove compartment. It looks like a can of nuts, but when he opens it a fake snake pops out. His son and wife have been dead for nineteen months, but he still has this can, the last thing his son bought from his favorite store, the Auburn Novelty Shop. He knows he should throw it out, but he can't bring himself to do it yet. Alan is an amateur magician, and Todd shared his father's love of tricks. His skill with magic is also evidence of his grace and agility.

King also introduces Alan's relationship with Polly. Alan decides to call her, just the sound of her voice will make him feel better. He recalls another event from his past, his connection to Thad Beaumont. We find out what happened to Thad after the events in *The Dark Half*. He has a drinking problem and is divorced. The failure of Thad's relationship leads Alan to blame himself for what happened to his own wife. He was too busy with others to see what was happening to her. The autopsy showed that Annie suffered from a brain tumor. Thad Beaumont's brain tumor was also the cause of his problems. When the Sheriff enters the police department we see him interact with First Deputy Norris Ridgewick. Alan operates according to what he sees as right. He can't know that telling Norris to give Danforth Keeton III a ticket for parking in the handicapped space will help create the chaos at the end of the novel. Buster's reaction sets off his personal disintegration and the destruction of the town. We last see Alan on the first day of the novel amusing himself by making shadow puppets on the wall.

The tricks and magic Alan plays with suggest that he has not lost his connection with childhood, an essential trait in a King hero. Alan may be haunted by the death of his wife and son, but he will briefly play the role of foster father for Brian Rusk's brother and uncover important clues about the first murderers in Castle Rock. Alan's role as a detective does not give him personal satisfaction because he cannot solve the mystery of his wife's death. He cannot understand why she was not wearing her seat belt, something she always did. His son was wearing his. He can't figure out if she was planning to commit suicide and wonders why she took their son with her. He blames himself for not seeing that something was wrong, and he also wonders if he could have done something to prevent it. He originally turned to Polly, his wife's friend, to see if she had any information to help him with this problem.

Alan is forced to deal with his ghosts as he attempts to prevent the destruction of the town. He tries to see a pattern in the inquiries he makes about what is happening. King reveals more about his character as we watch him try to solve the town's mysteries. He finally understands when he questions Brian's brother Sean after Brian's suicide. Sean reveals that Brian bought a baseball card he thought was a Sandy Koufax. When Sean saw it was just a dirty old card, Brian discovered the real truth about Gaunt. Sean tells Alan that Brian knew Gaunt wasn't really a man. Alan thinks he knows everything. On the way back to town he worries about why he didn't want his son to buy the trick can with the snake. He finally understands that the can would also appeal to Gaunt. It is a trick based on misdirection. Alan understands that misdirection is the key to the tricks Gaunt has others perform. He understands that magic can entertain, but it can also be used to make people angry with each other.

Alan only thinks he understands Gaunt. When he confronts him, Gaunt has left him a videotape of his wife's accident. Alan cannot stop himself from watching it. Polly forces him to see he has been tricked. Gaunt's version is flawed because in it Annie is wearing her seat belt. When Alan realizes this error he finally can confront Gaunt. He uses the snake in the can and the flower bouquet to win over Gaunt, who believes in magic. For a moment he thinks the snake is real, and it bites him. Gaunt drops his valise, and Alan is able to grab it. When they confront each other Alan creates shadow puppets of the town's past, the town's ghosts, to chase Gaunt. Sparrows from *The Dark Half*, a Saint Bernard from *Cujo,* and the sun dog from the story of that name all appear. Alan understands the importance of magic: it connects him to his dead son, to belief in illusion. He knows his magic is not misdirection, and he defeats Gaunt. As the survivors leave town Alan knows he will never really learn how his wife and child died, but he can finally accept this fact.

## Polly Chalmers

Polly Chalmers, too, must come to certain understandings before she can work with Alan to defeat Gaunt. Polly is a different kind of female character for King. His few positive female characters are usually identified with motherly activities; for example, Fran is pregnant for most of *The Stand.* Polly's secret relates to her motherhood. She was a single parent and left Castle Rock to have the child. After her father rejected her she was too proud to accept any help from her parents and eventually moved to San Francisco. She is still too proud to tell Alan what happened to her son. His baby-sitter caused a fire in Polly's apartment which killed them both. Gaunt uses this secret, forging a letter suggesting that Alan is looking into her past by making inquiries of the San Francisco Department of Child Welfare. Polly may feel guilty about her past, but King does not seem to judge her. She runs her own business, is compassionate in hiring Nettie, who was in a mental institution for killing her abusive husband, and has a settled, independent life. Like Alan, she works well with others, especially her employees. Aside from the one secret, she has a mature, adult relationship with Alan.

Her one great problem is her arthritis. Her motive for allowing Gaunt to control her is much more justified than that of the other characters. She is one of the last to deal with Gaunt and only does so because nothing helps the terrible pain in her hands. King also suggests that she is not thinking as clearly as she might because of the pain and the medicine she is taking to deal with it. Gaunt gives her a charm which takes away the pain. But in payment she plants information which turns Ace Merrill against Alan and almost causes her death. She may initially accept Gaunt's forged evidence, but she is finally able to see through it. Through a mental conversation with her Aunt Evvie, another independent woman, she discovers the forgery. When she was alive Aunt Evvie gave her advice and approved of her attempts to free herself from her parents and the town. Polly realizes that in the forged letter she is called Patricia.

In San Francisco she used the name Polly. When she frees herself of Gaunt's influence she also finally liberates herself from her past, from her pride and her hurt. Her freedom leads her to understand Gaunt. She is able to make Alan see as well. She knows she has to accept the pain of living, the pain in her arthritic hands. King also suggests that those who form lasting relationships based on trust will survive.

### Brian Rusk

Brian is another of the young boys who have important roles in King novels. While Brian shares some of their characteristics, he differs in important ways. He is still at the point where he maintains the beliefs of childhood. In many King novels this ability to retain a sense of wonder is what saves a child from destruction. Unfortunately for Brian, his belief in fantasy makes him a perfect subject for Gaunt, who uses Brian's imagination immediately. Brian senses Noah's Ark in a splinter of wood. He sees the baseball card he is supposed to see rather than the one Gaunt really gives him. Even when he finally forces himself to do the pranks Gaunt demands, he begins to enjoy them the way a child would. But Brian also quickly discovers that part of the joy in having a special card is showing it to others. He senses that this would get him in trouble because he could not explain how he got the card. He moves from enjoying to the more private pleasure of gloating. This reaction alters his personality as he closes up to others.

Brian realizes that Gaunt has trapped him, but he cannot find a way out. He sees no choice but to follow Gaunt's orders. He can't deal with the result of his actions, the deaths of Wilma and Nettie. He has no one who can help him. He is certain that someone saw him, and the Sheriff will be after him. Alan does try to talk to him, but Brian is losing his childhood. He does not react to Alan's flower trick. Brian can't confess, but he doesn't lie either. He tells Alan that a monster caused the destruction at Wilma's house. Alan cannot reach him. Brian's dreams have turned from his crush on his teacher to nightmares about the monster. He knows more than he wants too. "It's like knowing how the magician does his tricks" (463). The knowledge of what is behind the magic belongs to the adult world, and Brian cannot cope with it. Alan does not understand how seriously Brian has been hurt by this knowledge. Sean tries to prevent his brother's suicide, but Brian finally shoots himself. He has moved into the pain of the adult world too quickly.

### Norris Ridgewick

While Norris is not one of the most important characters in *Needful Things,* he is one of the few survivors. He has been a deputy for a while and worked with Alan investigating Homer Gamache's death in *The Dark Half.* Our first meeting with him in this book is not very impressive. He does not want to give Buster a parking ticket. We can tell he does not want to confront this man. While Alan likes him, he also makes the shadow hand puppet version of him "skinny and a little self-important" (67). Norris drives Alan crazy because he insists on changing into his uniform in the men's room. But he does stand up to Buster even though it ruins his day. At the end of that day he is trapped by Gaunt when he sees in the shop window a fishing rod like the one he used to have as a boy. He wants it because it represents the good times he had with his father.

Norris becomes involved in the violence in two ways. Like Polly, he cannot avoid performing his little prank. He even is at the point of suicide like Brian. But as he stands with the noose around his neck an inner voice forces him to face the truth. His fishing rod is just junk. He still almost dies. He is certain Gaunt has pushed him. But he manages to free himself in all senses of the word. He destroys the rod and goes after Gaunt. While Norris tries to arrest Ace and Buster, Ace shoots him. Norris survives and redeems himself, managing to shoot Ace before Ace can shoot Polly. Alan tells his First Deputy he can change his clothes in the men's room anytime. Norris still feels that all of the destruction is his fault. But Polly shows him how they are all to blame. The town no longer exists, but the survivors have learned to accept reality.

## THEME

In *Needful Things* King explores three familiar themes, managing to develop them in new ways: the relationship between the individual and the community, the importance of childhood, and the destructive impact of an evil presence. While some might only see the novel as an exposé of the greed of a community, not everyone in Castle Rock acts from the same motives or has the same desires. People may promise anything to acquire their needful things, but many of their purchases are not intrinsically valuable. Gaunt exploits people's desires, but these desires are often connected to simple dreams such as owning a certain baseball card or a beautiful piece of glass. The chosen items represent the hidden dreams of the owners and often suggest unfulfilled desires in their lives—a fishing rod like the one a father owned, or sunglasses owned by Elvis. But King is concerned about how far people will go to fulfill their desires. He is concerned that our quest for personal gratification can destroy society.

King is interested in both individual actions and the organization of the community. By taking apart Castle Rock he investigates what held it together. In *The Stand* King looks at what happens after a civilization is destroyed. In *Needful Things* he details the process of destruction. King uses Gaunt and his store to test the rules of society. He details the laws covering the behavior of the town toward a new store. But these codes are not strong enough to save the community. Kings shows how these codes break down. We quickly believe the worst of each other and act rather than talk. In part, we are trapped by our own needful things. We want to believe we can get what we want without paying the full price. Civilization is just a thin coating over our more violent impulses. Only a few of Gaunt's customers can see how they have been manipulated. King is not very hopeful about our ability to live together.

When the social structures of Castle Rock begin to fall apart, King shows how ineffective the traditional supports of a community can be. All the organizations we trust to maintain society become involved in the destruction. The Sheriff's office becomes a source of contamination when Norris falls under Gaunt's spell. Buster's actions compromise the city government, and the churches generate much of the hostility in town. When individuals begin to attack each other there is no higher organization to prevent the violence from escalating. King does not see much hope for society. In the end the town is destroyed and only a few individuals remain. Society's failure to control evil means that Gaunt survives to continue his work elsewhere. Alan can save the souls of his town, but we don't know if individuals in the next town will be able to save themselves. Alan can trick Gaunt because he has special powers of his own. He understands the power of magic and misdirection. Polly is able to get Alan away from the false video because of the force of their relationship. But King leaves us wondering what might have happened if these two people had not been successful. And they cannot save everyone. Many of Gaunt's victims are good people who just wanted to fulfill one of their dreams. The failure of the community in *Needful Things* allows Gaunt to partially succeed. He does not get their souls, but he does destroy Castle Rock. In King's world the punishment does not always fit the crime, and bad things can happen to good people. But society's rules do not protect good people who make bad decisions.

In *Needful Things* King changes his view of childhood. Even children are taken in by Gaunt. Their innocence is no protection. Brian sees the reality of his actions too late. His has lost the protection of being a child. In other King novels children survive because they believe in the monsters adults deny. Brian's childhood dream of owning a special baseball card betrays him. King may be suggesting that collecting baseball cards has become tainted by adult greed and materialism. Baseball cards have become big business. Brian is too young for the adult world. He has confused childhood desires with adult dreams of getting something for nothing. He cannot confide in Alan. He commits suicide, an act associated with adults, because he does not see any other solution.

Society's failure in *Needful Things* extends to the parent/child relationship. Alan does not really get a chance to form a new father/son relationship with Brian and save him. Gaunt's actions either play on failed father/son relationships or destroy potential relationships. Characters are drawn to Gaunt's shop by the promise of either improving or regaining a connection with a father figure. Brian's father started his collection. Brian has worked hard to get many of his cards, but the Sandy Koufax card is beyond his reach. A purchase from Gaunt's shop does not improve his relationship with his father because the terms of purchase make it impossible for Brian to share it with anyone. Items from Gaunt's shop isolate people because they cannot admit what they have done to purchase their treasures. Norris and Brian finally realize that things cannot substitute for true parent/child relationships. They feel so guilty about their actions that they no longer want to live. The destruction of family connections is just one kind of evil that Gaunt brings to Castle Rock.

Gaunt embodies a kind of evil which exists outside of normal human interactions. He is a monster, but he uses human needs and emotions as the tools of his destruction. In *Needful Things* King is saying good-bye to more than Castle Rock. He examines the nature of the relationship between good and evil in a small New England town. The opening description of the town explains its social structure and examines members of Castle Rock and the motives for their actions. King assigns different values to the choices people make in Gaunt's shop. The objects they select reflect their lives. Some people operate out of greed and pettiness. They choose things which support their fantasies. King finds these adults ridiculous and even dangerous. While Cora Rusk indulges in her fantasy relationship with Elvis, Brian, her son, commits suicide. Some shoppers are pathetic. Gaunt tempts Nettie with a piece of carnival glass. She once had gone crazy and killed her abusive husband when he broke pieces of her collection. King suggests that our attachment to things as a substitute for real relationships is sad, leading us to overvalue things and become paranoid about losing them.

Gaunt's evil is successful because he knows how to take small human defects and connect them to create mass destruction. No one really enjoys their purchase from Gaunt. His bargains are too costly. People can't show their objects to others. In most cases, if they shared the joy in their purchase, they would find out how they had been cheated. Gaunt controls the way they see their objects. They can't see the reality behind their bargains. Many of their treasures are really junk. False things cannot replace real relationships, as many people discover. They also realize that they have made bad bargains they can't revoke. Only a few people successfully break away from Gaunt's control. Alan escapes from the power of the videotape, and Polly returns her charm.

Alan is able to defeat Gaunt because he is not impressed with the man or his power. Alan's character unites many of the themes in the novel. He has lost his son and cannot save Brian. He is a representative of law and order who cannot prevent the destruction of the town. But Alan survives and triumphs because he learns how to accept his losses. His dead son's trick works on Gaunt. His successful relationship with Polly overcomes the power of Gaunt's tape. Their combined goodness turns Alan's magic tricks into real snakes and shafts of light which overcome Gaunt's evil. Gaunt is not destroyed, but he leaves town without the souls he came for. The survivors know they will have to live with the consequences of their actions. There will be no more Castle Rock. But they value what they have learned. They see the effect of the evil Gaunt represents, and they understand their own complicity in the destruction. This knowledge is their punishment for agreeing to Gaunt's terms, but it also gives them the power to avoid such choices in the future.

## ALTERNATIVE READING: GENRE

*Needful Things* is another example of how King explores the limits of the horror genre in his recent fiction. In *Misery* he uses realism to create a different kind of horror—one without supernatural origins. In this novel we must witness the horror of human evil. *Gerald's Game* and *Dolores Claiborne* are also realistic novels. In *Needful Things* King examines our relationship to the supernatural. He looks at the horror genre and its relationship to the evil which comes from within us and that which has a source outside of us. Many of King's horror novels deal with evil which originates outside of the individual: the aliens in *Tommyknockers,* the clown in *It,* the ghosts in *The Shining.* Often the horror comes from inside a character. In *Needful Things* the evil begins outside of the individual, but humans carry out the destruction. Gaunt uses human malice and greed to accomplish his destruction.

In the horror genre, we expect a conflict which will involve some aspect of the supernatural. We also assume that there will be a certain amount of violence connected to this conflict and that the conflict will include a confrontation between good and evil. Like other King novels, *Needful Things* has all these elements of the genre. Gaunt is like many supernatural horror figures in his fiction. He controls people through a kind of hypnosis, appearing to them when they think they are alone. He knows things about people that no one else knows. He operates out of a sense of pure evil. Humans amuse him, and he plays with them. At the end of the novel he reveals his true nature. As he leaves town in defeat he goes through a series of changes. We don't always see Gaunt, but his car turns into a buckboard driven by a dwarf and then a medicine-show wagon with the sign "Caveat Emptor," buyer beware. As he leaves, the souls he has captured escape from the valise, and the town and its people are no longer poisoned. The fighting and the storm stop.

King expands the genre by including more than just the horror which comes from outside. He is also interested in the way we contribute to the horror we experience. Gaunt exploits the needs of the citizens of Castle Rock. He may have an unfair advantage because of his supernatural powers, but he cannot be effective without their help. The destruction he helps them create may have started because of his supernatural powers. But Castle Rock is destroyed by human violence. King uses Alan's interest in magic to help explain what is happening. Magic works because the audience is tricked into believing. The magician misdirects us. When Alan understands this concept he understands how Gaunt operates. But magic is so powerful that we may fall under its spell even if we know there's a trick. Alan falls under Gaunt's spell until Polly helps him see Gaunt's mistake. Alan's magic is human in origin, but it becomes transformed when he meets Gaunt. Contact with Gaunt releases the supernatural in others. Gaunt believes in the power of magic, and his belief turns human magic into the supernatural.

In *Needful Things* King explores the relationship between the supernatural and natural worlds. He is concerned not just with the horror we usually find in the genre. He is worried about the natural horror which results from the way humans treat each other. He looks back on the past of Castle Rock. Some of the town's problems have a supernatural origin, as in the monster dog released by the photographs in "The Sun Dog." Other conflicts in Castle Rock may combine natural and supernatural forces. In *The Dead Zone* special powers lead to the discovery of a serial killer. In this novel individuals are responsible for the human horror. Cujo is just a poor rabid dog who attacks the humans and causes the death of a child. The supernatural is not really important in *Cujo*. Thad Beaumont does not wish his evil half to come alive in *The Dark Half*, and Thad needs help from supernatural forces to overcome him. In *Needful Things* a single evil being sets the townspeople against each other. Gaunt accomplishes some of his goal by using the evil in us all. King still employs supernatural elements to explore the horror genre in this novel. But he also suggests that human horror is more destructive than any which comes from outside of us. Castle Rock has been the scene of both natural and supernatural horror. King has used this town as a setting to examine the many kinds of evil possible in the horror novel. He finally destroys the town by combining the power of a supernatural evil with the destructive power of the average human being.

# 9

# *Insomnia*
## (1994)

Although King wrote *Insomnia* in 1990, it was not published until 1994. In an interview King indicated that it was a completed novel of about 550 pages. "It's no good. I know it's not publishable. And I've been writing and publishing books for a long time. . . . And maybe some day you'll read it, but it won't be for a long time" (Beahm, *Stephen King Story* 244–45). The final version is 787 pages long. We don't know what King added to the original draft to change his mind about publishing it, but *Insomnia* is an important novel in his development as an author. Throughout his career King has created characters often ignored by both mainstream and genre fiction, such as blue collar workers, the unemployed, and those on the margins of society. Like *Dolores Claiborne*, it examines the lives of older people. In both works the central characters are people we do not usually think of as heroic. Dolores Claiborne is a sixty-five-year-old housekeeper. In *Insomnia*, Ralph Roberts is seventy and a recent widower and Lois Chasse is sixty-eight and a widow. Together they perform heroic actions with wide-ranging consequences for characters in King's fictional world.

*Insomnia's* explorations of fictional time and its examination of different genres mark another important development in King's work. In this novel King departs from real time to present different temporal periods which exist in a world beyond human time schemes. Playing with time is not usual in the horror genre. Although characters often move back and forth between the real world and an imaginary world, the action is generally presented chronologically. Horror also uses elements of the supernatural to involve the reader in a fictional universe connected both to our own world and to a world of the imagination. *Insomnia* is set in Derry, a fictional town associated with some of King's horror novels, especially *It*. The horror genre creates an atmosphere where supernatural, terrifying events are possible. In King's novels places like Derry become associated with unnatural events. In *Insomnia* many of these events move beyond a narrow definition of the supernatural. While we think that supernatural events can't really occur in our world, some people believe that the strange visions experienced in *Insomnia* may actually exist.

*Insomnia*'s story is also connected to the fantasy genre of stories about quests for magical objects to help the hero save the world. In fantasy novels characters may travel in time. *Insomnia* moves from the present into the future, and its characters move from human time to a higher plane where time passes more quickly. *Insomnia*'s ending relates it directly to another kind of King novel—the volumes of *The Dark Tower* series. The quest Ralph and Lois are told to pursue results in their saving an individual who is to become important in *The Dark Tower* series. By its end *Insomnia* moves from being just a horror novel to one which crosses many genre boundaries.

## PLOT DEVELOPMENT AND NARRATIVE STRUCTURE

*Insomnia* is organized like many King novels. It begins with a prologue, "Winding the Deathwatch." The main body of the work is divided into three parts: "Little Bald Doctors," "The Secret City," and "The Crimson King." The novel ends with an epilogue, "Winding the Deathwatch (II)." Each section is introduced with a drawing and selections of poetry or prose. The prologue describes the death of Ralph's first wife, Carolyn, from a brain tumor. Ralph hears a death watch ticking as he sees his wife decline. The prologue also explores a single puzzling incident during this period. Ralph takes a walk every day as a way of dealing with his own anxieties about Carolyn's condition. He is near the airport when he sees an automobile accident involving one of his neighbors, Ed Deepneau. Ed drives out an airport gate into the path of a truck, causing a collision. After the accident he acts in a very paranoid manner, becoming violent and using language Ralph has never associated with him. Ed accuses the victim of the crash, a man who works for a landscaping company, of carrying dead babies in his truck. The man finally opens a bag of fertilizer to prove his innocence. Ralph gets a ride home with another friend, and they both notice the Japanese lettering on the scarf Ed is wearing.

King gives only this partial information, failing to provide fuller explanation until later in the novel. During the next section we keep wondering about these puzzles along with Ralph. The section opens with the first symptoms of Ralph's progressive insomnia. He wakes earlier and earlier each day. Gradually we understand that Ralph's problems go beyond normal insomnia.

We begin to notice other events as we follow Ralph on his walks. A conflict is growing in Derry between those who believe in a woman's right to abortion and those who see abortion as murder. Ralph visits a friend's shop and signs a petition to bring Susan Edwina Day, an activist, to town. Another store across the street already has an anti-Day poster in its window. Gradually King provides pieces of information. We sense that these details are important, but we have no idea where to place them. It is like opening a large jigsaw puzzle and beginning to sort out the pieces. We learn about a woman's clinic called WomanCare and about Charlie Pickering's attempt to firebomb it. We meet Ralph's friends, Bill McGovern, who lives downstairs, and Lois Chasse, a widow.

In the midst of these seemingly purposeless events Ralph has to deal with another kind of crisis at the grocery store. Ralph sees Helen Deepneau, a battered woman, trying to get to the store. She is bloody and can barely carry her baby, Natalie. Ralph runs out of the store and manages to catch Natalie just as she falls out of Helen's arms. Helen explains that Ed hit her because she signed a petition to bring Susan Day to Derry.

As the police arrive Ralph goes to confront Ed. When he approaches the Deepneau house he hears a song from an old album. Grace Slick is singing the chorus from "White Rabbit," about pills that change your size. This reference both to the song and to *Alice in Wonderland* will reappear later in the novel. Ralph understands that Ed must have been crazy for some time. Ed tells Ralph that Helen joined the Centurions and the Crimson King when she signed the petition. He repeats the accusations he made after his automobile accident about dead babies being hauled away in trucks covered with tarps. Ed's description of the Crimson King resembles the kind of figure frequently used to embody evil in Stephen King's fiction. He often personifies evil as a supernatural being with human traits. According to Ed, the Crimson King is a shape changer who is looking for the Messiah to destroy him. Ralph is just as puzzled as we are about this information. We think Ed is just crazy. Ed also mentions how the world can be full of colors. At this point we share Ralph's perspective, hearing but not understanding.

Ralph's insomnia worsens, and it does not respond to any treatment. One day while talking to Bill and Lois he has his first experience seeing auras. Auras "surround human beings, chiefly encircling the head, and are supposed to proceed from the nervous system." Auras can contain many colors and cannot be seen by physical sight (*Encyclopedia of Occultism and Parapsychology,* s.v. "aura"). We may remember Ed's remarks about colors and connect them to these images. At first King does not explain exactly what Ralph sees when he notices colors which seem to surround people. Readers who are aware of auras might guess what Ralph is seeing. For the rest of us, King introduces these extraordinary visions gradually so that we are convinced of their reality along with Ralph. Ralph is afraid to discuss what he sees with anyone because people are so ready to label older people senile.

Joe Wyzer, a sympathetic druggist, discusses Ralph's symptoms and explains his experiences as hyper reality, an increase in sensory awareness caused by insomnia. Joe's function is to give a realistic explanation for these phenomena, helping us believe that such events could occur under the right circumstances. Ralph is no longer frightened by what he sees now that he attributes it to his sleeplessness. Next, King must make both Ralph and the reader believe in auras.

The next stage is for Ralph to meet someone else who sees auras. Ed warns Ralph about getting involved in things which are too deep for him. Ed asks him if he sees the colors, and tells Ralph he will have to answer to the little bald doctor if he interferes in Ed's business again. Ralph dismisses Ed's conversation as the ranting of a madman. Once more we do not know how to deal with the information. King moves us back to a frightening encounter in the real world, but he also keeps us aware of undercurrents which make us uneasy about the supernatural world we keep encountering.

Finally, one night Ralph does see two little bald doctors go into a neighbor's house. He calls the police, who find her dead of natural causes. There is no evidence of a break-in. King carefully describes how Ralph sees these men. We do not doubt his vision, but suspect that they may not be a part of our world. One carries stainless steel scissors, not the tools of the normal burglar. Ralph sees that their auras are not like those of humans. He feels that his vision is confirmed when Rosalie, the neighborhood stray dog, sniffs the tracks left by their auras. We also tend to believe the instincts of an animal.

Ralph watches a third bald doctor going after Rosalie. They communicate telepathically. The doctor uses the same type of language Ed used at the airport. Ralph manages to deflect the doctor from attacking Rosalie this time. Ralph learns that Lois's son and daughter-in-law want to put her into a retirement home because she has told her doctor about having insomnia and seeing auras. When she confides in Ralph, he finally believes all of his experiences. King has brought us to the point where we accept that they can see such things.

Ralph finally understands that the bald doctors use the scissors to cut the cords of the balloon-shaped auras we all have connected to our bodies. Our auras indicate our health and mood to those who see them. When the cord is cut we will die in the near future. Ralph and Lois work together to find out what is happening to them and to Derry. Their union is both intellectual and romantic. Ralph realizes that there are differences between the two bald doctors who work together and the one with the rusty scalpel who attacked Rosalie. But he also knows they are all supernatural beings. He still doesn't understand how they might be connected to the Centurions Ed mentioned. He links these fantasy characters to others from Tolkien's fantasy *The Lord of the Rings*. He relates this trilogy to his experiences even more closely later in the novel.

Two of the bald doctors explain many of the events of the novel to Ralph and Lois. They tell the couple that they must prevent Ed from killing an individual whose death would alter the higher Purpose of the world. Ralph and Lois cannot figure out exactly who they are to save. They are told that it is not Susan Day, but that unless they act the person will be killed at her rally that night.

King does not let us know any more than Ralph and Lois, but we do learn a few more important clues with them. Ralph learns that the Japanese letters on Ed's scarf form the word "kamikaze." We figure out that Ed is going to become a kamikaze pilot and bomb the civic center during the rally that night. We now know why he was coming from the direction of the flying school at the beginning of the novel. Ralph and Lois also recognize the Japanese word's ironic meaning—"divine wind." Ed is a suicide pilot with what he sees as a holy mission even though he might kill many innocent people.

Gradually all of the people in the story begin to come together. Events get more and more complex as the rally approaches. Ralph and Lois are drawn in various directions as they try to figure out how to prevent the destruction they see coming. Finally they discover the home of the third bald doctor, Atropos, in a hole next to a tree. Their descent into the hole recalls other fantasies, making us think of Alice falling down the hole into Wonderland and the hobbit's home in *The Lord of the Rings*. King includes a reference to Bluebeard's wife entering a forbidden room, which he also uses in *The Shining*. Ralph and Lois do not know what they are looking for, but they see Atropos's trophies, including Gage Creed's sneaker from *Pet Sematary*, a reference to another King novel. They finally find a death bag containing objects taken from living people who could become victims at the civic center. Ralph cuts open the bag and sees Ed's wedding ring. Remembering lines about one ring which controls all from *The Lord of the Rings*, he grabs it. King provides one final reference. Another ring appears in place of the ring Ralph removes, and he thinks of *The Five Hundred Hats of Bartholomew Cubbins* by Dr. Seuss. In this story, each time Bartholomew removes a hat another appears.

Atropos shows Ralph a future event hidden from us and Lois. King introduces this new tension near the resolution of the major conflict in the novel to balance Ralph's actions which affect history with those which are more personal. Ralph and Lois still do not really understand their mission, and the rally is about to start. Ralph has used Atropos, the name of one of the three fates of Greek mythology, for the evil doctor. The other two, who have no real names, suggest they can be called Clotho and Lachesis after the two remaining fates. These doctors finally explain that they must save a special boy who will be at the rally: *"If the child dies, the Tower of all existence will fall, and the consequences of such a fall are beyond your comprehension. And beyond ours, as well"* (683). Ralph agrees to attempt to stop Ed, but he makes a trade. The two doctors perform an operation on Ralph's arm, severing the Bracelets of Fortune at his wrist. King may be referring to palmistry; the rings where the wrist connects to the arm are called Bracelets of Life (*Encyclopedia of Occultism and Parapsychology*, s.v. "palmistry"). The wound heals, and Ralph sets out to fulfill his promise.

Ralph, by moving to a different level of time, transports himself into Ed's plane. Through this action, he grows large enough to reach the plane in the sky. Ralph recalls the words from "White Rabbit" he heard the day he went to confront Ed. He wears Ed's wedding ring as he battles Ed and the Crimson King. King brings together all of the pieces he has presented throughout the novel. Several visions appear to Ralph, who finally feels that he is in the court of the Crimson King. Lois calls to him telepathically to help him. When the Crimson King sinks his fangs into his arm, Ralph is able to trigger the booby trap Clotho and Lachesis planted. The King is blown away, but Ralph is still left in the plane with Ed, who is starting his descent to crash into the civic center. Ralph gets the controls away from Ed and brings the plane down just short of the civic center. Susan Day is killed, but the boy, Patrick Danville, is saved. He too has the book about Bartholomew Cubbins, the boy who can't take off his hat. He has been drawing a picture of the Red King, Roland, and a dark tower.

The end of this section and the epilogue connect all the remaining pieces of the plot. Ralph and Lois finally sleep normally. They marry and have several good years. They even get a dog named Rosalie. When Ralph begins to hear the same death watch he heard when Carolyn was dying, he knows he is about to fulfill his bargain with the doctors. We watch, finally understanding that he agreed to trade his life for Natalie's. Ralph dies saving her from being hit by a car. As he dies the scar disappears from his arm. The novel ends as it began, with an automobile accident, but much has changed. Rather than a circle, *Insomnia* is shaped like a spiral. Ralph dies, but new worlds open up to us. We still have questions, some of which the ending answers. We now understand some of the things Ralph did earlier. Our world moves along without real endings, and King closes the novel by leaving an important question open. We do not know why it is so important for one young boy to live. We have reached a stopping point in his examination of the worlds he has created, but we have a long way to go to reach the Dark Tower and the answers we will find there.

## CHARACTERS

As is often the case in King's fiction, the plot dominates *Insomnia*. While there are many characters in *Insomnia,* and the novel deals with events that determine the course of King's world, only two characters are fully developed, Lois and Ralph. Ralph is the most important character. Lois, while also important, does not become a significant character until more than a third of the way into the story. King tells much of the story from Ralph's point of view. We see most of the characters from his perspective.

Aside from Lois and Ralph, the other significant characters in the novel mainly work to keep the plot going. While Ed is certainly an important force in terms of the action, we meet him only at key points. The bald doctors and the Crimson King also move the plot along and are important thematically. But King deliberately does not develop them as characters, using them as nonhuman agents of good and evil. The other humans who appear work with the plot. It is easy to see how King uses Helen and Natalie to get Ralph involved in the world connected with Susan Day's appearance in Derry. Dorrance is an agent of the Purpose, and he gets Joe to help him. Bill helps Lois and Ralph get together.

### Lois Chasse

Lois has a certain amount of independence. But we seldom view her apart from her relationship with Ralph. Her presentation is interesting, especially since King novels tend to have few fully developed women. Lois is a rare fictional older woman. She is brave, intelligent, loving, and sensible. She does get tired and frightened at times, but she does not run from her fears. At the end she is critical to Ralph's victory over Ed. She is willing to get involved with Ralph on all levels. King deals honestly and kindly with their sexual relationship and their growing love. They acknowledge their former spouses at the same time they form this new union. But we never get to know Lois at the same level we know Ralph. We don't share her experience as she suffers from insomnia. We learn the story of her encounter with her son and daughter-in-law only when she tells it to Ralph.

### Ralph Roberts

Ralph is the real focus of the story and its most fully developed character. We see what he eats and wears. We know he isn't concerned about show. A friend comments about his torn shirt, but he does not run to change it. King shows us a lot about Ralph, but we know little about his past. He was a salesman who had a bit of a drinking problem. Despite his age he resembles King's children in some ways. He is afraid to believe what he sees, fearing people will think him senile. He is more concerned about how he appears to others for the same reason. Ralph is able to discover the hidden world of the children of Derry and is tuned in to the supernatural events which surface there. Like many children in

King's work, Ralph learns much about the world but does not really grow during the course of the novel.

Ralph finds worlds he has not imagined as the novel progresses. King suggests that he is chosen by the Purpose because of what he is. He is old enough to return to the visions of childhood. He will be able to see and understand the auras. But he has the wisdom and strength to deal with the challenges he must face. In Ralph, King presents the perfect hero. He has the world view of a child and the maturity of an adult. King needs a new kind of hero because Ralph does not encounter the traditional monsters of the horror novel. He deals with a world which seems to be falling apart without falling apart himself. He then must deal with forces beyond human experience. Unlike the traditional hero, who needs strength and endurance, Ralph needs the mental toughness to deal with the knowledge he discovers. He also has to be able to accept help from others.

## THEME

If King develops a new kind of hero in *Insomnia,* he also explores different ideas. All of the themes in the novel relate to the idea of insomnia and the effects of sleeplessness. Insomnia induces a state of heightened awareness in the characters, leading them to understand the everyday world and its underlying organization in new ways. Ralph and Lois's experiences lead us into a complex analysis of these themes; King wants us to see our world differently and to believe in a world beyond our everyday perception. While King wants to show us things we may not be aware of, he connects his new ideas to themes explored in other works, including the interaction of the individual and society and the importance of retaining the imaginative experience of childhood when we grow up.

Early in the novel we watch Ralph cope with insomnia. He does not understand until later that this sleeplessness is his path to a deeper vision of the world around him. King examines the world of older people, looking at how the individual deals with the aging process and how the community of older people operates. He has explored the relationship between the individual and the community in many of his novels. In this novel Ralph lives in a special world—the world of the retired. The members of his community work well together. They care for each other, worry when one of them is absent, support each other in life and in death. Their world is separate from that of younger people. They have less money, and they need less. They interact with the world around them even though most other people ignore them. Ralph's strongest contacts with people outside of his group are with Helen and Natalie, who are also outsiders. Ralph's awareness of his community helps him see the other communities which exist in Derry.

King shows that some communities work when they are made up of a small group of people with the same needs and goals. The larger world of working adults is split into two major camps—those who support a woman's right to abortion and those who oppose it. Even in this world values and people survive when they work together. Helen would not have found a new life without Ralph and without the members of WomanCare. Destruction and evil come from individuals who act on their own outside of the normal boundaries of society.

Later in the novel, "The Secret City" section begins with Ralph suddenly recognizing that different Derrys exist for special groups. He sees the children's Derry, a world usually below adult view. He realizes that the old folks' city is also ignored by other adults. Ralph walks to the spot near the airport where retirees meet, talk, and play chess. He understands that much of what the older population does is unnoticed by the rest of the adults in Derry. Ralph and Lois often use this awareness as a means of working toward their goals in the novel. They can move through town without being noticed by officials who might question the presence of younger people. King uses the increased awareness of insomnia to show how our vision of the world is limited. We begin to understand that we are aware of only a very small part of our world.

King then uses Ralph and Lois to lead us into a world beyond our daily experience and beyond our expectations for the horror genre. Some people may believe in auras and be able to see them, but most don't. The world of parapsychology represented by auras is quite different from anything King usually presents. The phenomena of parapsychology are not part of the imaginary world of the horror novel. While most people do not believe vampires exist, many do believe in the reality of auras. Their ability to see auras leads Ralph and Lois to a much deeper understanding of their world. While the supernatural can take characters to places beyond their normal experience, it does not usually lead to a different comprehension of the universe. The characters in *It* go beneath the town of Derry to find the source of its horror, but they do not learn about the organization of the world from the monster they find.

King paces the action so that we follow Ralph and Lois as they explore the powers they have gained and learn how to use them. We also have a chance to believe in these changes. By presenting them as extensions of real situations, King makes these experiences credible. Once Ralph and Lois begin to understand auras, King introduces the bald doctors, who are also visible because of insomnia. We follow as Ralph gradually figures out their function in the world. Even if we do not totally believe, we want to. When Ralph and Lois see one bald doctor finally get Rosalie's aura, they actually observe the effect of severing a life. Rosalie is accidentally hit and killed by Joe Wyzer. The bald doctor looks at the couple and gloats. In another encounter with this new vision they are disturbed to see that their friend Bill's aura is now black, a sign he will die soon.

King uses the doctors to develop ideas about destiny and the organization of the universe. Ralph and Lois finally meet the other two doctors, who are associated with the three Fates who, in Greek and Roman mythology, control human destiny. In Greek mythology they are three sisters, the Moerae, whose names are identified with their functions. Clotho spins the thread of life; Lachesis sets the length of the thread, and Atropos cuts it (*Harper's Dictionary of Classical Literature and Antiquities*, s.v. "Moerae"). King changes the Fates into men and alters their functions slightly. The two men say that they can be called Clotho and Lachesis. Ralph gives the name of the third fate, Atropos, to the absent doctor with the rusty scalpel who has killed Rosalie. The two doctors take them up to another level of time and existence usually hidden from short timers to explain what is happening to them and to their world. They use some of the same terms Roland uses in *The Dark Tower* series.

Clotho and Lachesis begin by explaining the relationship between freedom of choice and destiny as a part of "ka, *the great wheel of being*" (461). There are four constants in the universe: "*Life, Death, the Purpose, and the Random*" (462). The two fates are agents of the Purpose, whose role is to bring people to a purposeful death at their time. The other doctor is an agent of the Random, and his work accounts for most of the senseless death in the world. Atropos cut the cord of someone who had no clear role, Ed Deepneau, and set in motion events which Ralph and Lois must work to prevent. Clotho and Lachesis have called on them to serve the higher Purpose. In *Insomnia* these explanations serve to introduce a view of how the universe is organized. Earlier, King explored these ideas in *The Dark Tower* series.

After Ralph and Lois save the child, we learn that "on all levels of the universe matters both Random and Purposeful resumed their ordained courses" (731). The narrator makes the final connection between this book and *The Dark Tower* series. "Worlds which had trembled for a moment in their orbits now steadied, and in one of those worlds, in a desert that was the apotheosis of all deserts, a man named Roland turned over in his bed roll" (731). King mentions no other characters from this series. In the course of the three novels Roland gains three companions. Since we have not yet met Patrick in *The Dark Tower* series, we can only assume that King is referring to a promised novel dealing with Roland's earlier life. Before they disappear from Ralph's and Lois's lives, Clotho and Lachesis tell them that the boy will save two men's lives. Roland is one of them. If he were to die, the balance between the Random and the Purpose would be destroyed.

In *Insomnia* King suggests a structure beyond the individual which organizes our lives. As we can see with Ralph, we still can exercise free will. But there is also a certain randomness to events. King has been concerned with the randomness of some evil, with the bad things that happen to good people. In this novel he uses the idea of the interaction of the Higher Purpose and the Random as a way of explaining these events. As in *The Dark Tower* series, the word "ka" represents the idea of our individual destinies, which "ka-tet" refers to the group we are bound to. Only small groups or individuals can make changes in the life of the individual or society as a whole. But their actions can affect the direction of the world for good or for evil.

King also examines the hero in *Insomnia*, suggesting that the traditional view of the hero is not the only way to look at this role. Rather than concentrating on externals, King shows us a hero who is strong because of the values he holds. Ralph is independent, but he uses this independence to serve the greater good and takes on a job without having to understand exactly what he must do. He accepts the idea of a mission, something which must be done for the greater good of society. At the end of the novel he also understands the idea of sacrifice when he gives up what is left of his life so that Natalie can live hers fully. In these roles he is contrasted with the hero he is helping to save, Roland of *The Dark Tower*, who is very much the traditional action hero. He combines elements of the gunfighter and the knight. In Roland's world this kind of hero is necessary. He spends part of his time turning people from our world into the right kind of hero for his. But King tells us that a different kind of hero is needed in our world. To fight the Crimson King, Ralph works through the world of his youth, the memories of his mother. And he wins only because he can also accept the assistance of a loved one, Lois.

## ALTERNATE READING: FEMINISM

A feminist reading of a work looks at how it deals with women and women's issues. The structure of a novel can also give the reader a positive or negative view of women. Novels with female characters who are active participants, controlling the action, or equal partners with men, present positive images of women. Some works present negative views by reinforcing stereotypical roles suggesting that women are incapable of controlling their lives. Novels may also reveal the oppression of women. How female characters are developed also affects whether they are presented positively or negatively. We judge these characters in the same way we deal with elements of the plot. In *Insomnia* King explores both the roles of women in society and the development of their characters.

King deals with a range of female actions in this novel. Lois is most crucial to the outcome of the plot. While she is not as important as Ralph in controlling the action in the novel, he would not be successful without her. At times she does not seem as strong as Ralph, especially when she has to look at something awful such as a death. Most of the time we see Lois through Ralph's eyes. When he sees her as physically attractive, that does not mean that King is judging women just by their looks. We also need to understand that King is trying to portray older people whose ideas about the relationships between men and women were developed at a different time. We have to be careful not to judge their attitudes too critically. We need to see Lois's character and actions in relation to King's presentation of the other women in this novel.

As the battered woman, Helen represents an ongoing concern of King's. Women who have been abused by their husbands in many of his novels. These women are always depicted sympathetically, and the abusers are usually punished. In *Insomnia* King makes a special point of showing how the laws in Maine do not keep Ed in jail after he batters Helen. While King feels that the legal system does not do a good job of handling this crime, he does present individuals who are concerned about the flaws in the system, for example, a policeman who wants better laws for abusers. He also shows women that there are alternatives, like the WomanCare group and the safe house Helen lives in. He presents the group's work with abused women very sympathetically. He uses Helen's reservations about going there as a means of demonstrating how the women help her to get out of an abusive relationship.

Some feminists might view King's presentation of another issue of importance to women as more questionable. Throughout *Insomnia* the town of Derry is increasingly divided into pro-abortion and anti-abortion camps. He shows the destructive side of the fanatics in both groups. He does not like the violence with which they present their views. Ralph is not a fanatic. When he signs the petition to bring Susan Day to town he does it because he thinks of Carolyn and what her attitude would have been. "*She was no fan of abortion, but she was also no fan of men coming home after the bars close and mistaking their wives for soccer balls*" (48). He knows she would also have signed because she would have liked to hear Susan Day out of intellectual curiosity. King does not like the way the abortion issue divides people into opposing groups. But he does suggest a difference in the groups. The WomanCare group is stubborn and risks death because they refuse to call off the rally. But the other group creates radical members like Ed, who wants to bomb the rally, and Charlie Pickering, who attacks Ralph and the WomanCare house. The most radical elements of both groups do not survive. Susan Day is killed by Ed's bomb even though most of the others are saved. King refuses to make an absolute stand because he does not like the extremes on either side. But he does support those who approach the issue rationally. And he makes an interesting point when he connects the issue of abortion to that of abuse. Ultimately he supports women's rights. He also presents more positive and complex images of women than he has in many of his earlier works.

# 10

# *Dolores Claiborne* (1993) and *Rose Madder* (1995)

Three of Stephen King's recent novels have women as central characters: *Gerald's Game* (1992), *Dolores Claiborne* (1993), and *Rose Madder* (1995). While all three deal with the abuse of women, they differ in their manipulation of the supernatural. *Gerald's Game* and *Dolores Claiborne* are connected by a solar eclipse and a shared telepathic vision. During the eclipse characters in each novel are involved in traumatic experiences and also see images of each other. While Jessie Burlingame's father molests her in *Gerald's Game* she has a vision of a woman leading her husband to a well. Dolores Claiborne, who is getting her husband into the well, has a vision of a young girl being molested by her father. Later in *Dolores Claiborne* Dolores senses that the adult Jessie is in trouble. Dolores's two visions are the only instances of the use of the supernatural in the novel. *Gerald's Game* suggests the possibility of other supernatural events, but these seem to be explained by the end of the novel. *Rose Madder* combines extremely realistic descriptions of wife beating with an extensive exploration of the supernatural. While all three novels are examples of the ways in which King challenges his readers with new techniques and themes, a comparison of the most traditional, *Rose Madder*, and the least, *Dolores Claiborne*, gives us an appreciation of recent developments in King's fiction.

## PLOT DEVELOPMENT AND NARRATIVE STRUCTURE

*Dolores Claiborne* and *Rose Madder* are examples of King's shorter, compact novels. Their plot structure differs from those of most of King's novels in that they present most of the action from a woman's point of view. *Dolores Claiborne* also introduces a dramatic change in King's customary organization of his fiction. King usually separates his novels into three to five large parts or books and further divides these into chapters. He may also include a prologue and an epilogue. *Dolores Claiborne* has no divisions of any kind in the body of the novel, although it does close with a "Scrapbook" of short articles. In this novel the title character has been accused of killing her employer, Vera Donovan. She goes to the police to tell her story, and the novel is the written record of that confession. *Rose Madder* has a slightly more traditional construction. It opens with a prologue and closes with an epilogue. The novel is divided into ten sections, each of which has a title, and each section contains several short chapters.

In both novels time is treated in complex ways. Dolores Claiborne begins by saying she hasn't decided how she will tell her story, "back to front or front to back" (4). She compromises by starting in the middle and working both ways, no matter what her listeners want. *Rose Madder* opens with a startling moment from Rosie's past and then moves ahead nine years. Once we get to the present, the story is organized chronologically except for the moments when we shift to the point of view of Norman Daniels, Rosie's husband. In these instances time overlaps as King retells the same event from the perspective of different characters.

### Dolores Claiborne

Character is more important than action in *Dolores Claiborne*. The events of the novel are not the source of its suspense. We believe Dolores when she says she's going to tell the truth. She immediately admits she killed her husband thirty years ago but denies killing Vera, her wealthy employer. She must tell the story of her relationship with these two people in order to explain both her guilt and innocence. The suspense comes from learning how and why she acted, rather than what she did. Throughout Dolores's story we hear only her voice. We can guess some of the reactions of her listeners by her responses, but we hear other people's conversation only from Dolores. She talks to Andy Bissette, the police chief, Frank Proulx, another policeman, and Nancy Bannister, the recorder. She comes from Little Tall Island, and life on an island is an important part of her story.

Once she gets beyond the preliminaries Dolores opens her story by setting the time. Just as anyone remembers dates by tying them to specific events, Dolores marks years in her life by significant events. She tells about her husband, Joe, and their three children, Selena, fifteen, Joe Junior, thirteen, and Little Pete, nine in 1963 when Joe died. The story moves back and forth in time as Dolores places Joe's murder three years after Vera's husband's death. She begins by connecting Joe's death with Vera's moving permanently to the island, where she had previously just summered. Joe left her no money to live on, so Dolores, who had previously worked summers for Vera, began to work for her full time. Vera's asking her to work full time seems casual at this point in the story. Later we learn of stronger connections between the deaths of the two husbands.

Dolores then describes her relationship with Vera from that period to the present and her shift from housekeeper to paid companion. As she describes events from the past, Dolores links the fact that other workers in the house heard her shouting at Vera with their suspicion that she killed Vera. She associates the gossip about Vera with the gossip about Joe's death. King uses the connection between two suspicious deaths to move back in time and uncover the reasons for her marriage to Joe, since she works for Vera because Joe does not provide for her. We jump forward as she tells us she wasn't worried about him laying his hands on her because that stopped in 1960 or 1961. From the way she makes that statement we suspect that while Joe may have been beating her he may also have been putting his hands on someone else in the family as a molester. King ties Dolores's acceptance of the beatings to her childhood, when her father beat her mother. We then find out why Joe no longer hit Dolores toward the end of his life. She tells of the confrontation she had with him which she won because he was really a coward. But in the interconnected chain of events forming the plot of this novel, winning this battle ultimately leads to her murder of Joe.

King presents the key events in Dolores's life in small pieces to keep us interested in learning more of the relevant details. He makes connections through associations in Dolores's mind rather than by means of chronological order. The movements back and forth in time show how events separated in time are connected. Selena witnesses the fight where Dolores triumphs over Joe and feels sorry for her father. Joe takes advantage of this sympathy by molesting her. When Dolores finds out, she makes him promise not to touch Selena any more. But she is worried about his effect on the children. Dolores does not know that Joe has decided to take revenge on her after she confronts him over Selena. She tries to withdraw the children's college savings from the bank, planning to leave Joe and move to Portland with the children. But Joe, having claimed that the passbooks were missing, has moved all the money into his own account. Dolores is trapped. She can't stand the way Joe looks at Selena or the way little Joe hates his father. This series of events, presented in chronological order, helps us understand how Dolores arrives at the point where she sees murder as her only option. King also wants us to remain sympathetic to Dolores.

Vera's contribution to this chain of events becomes clear when she shows Dolores an article about the solar eclipse which will cover part of Maine in July 1963. Vera suggests that a fatal accident might be the solution. Any money left over after he spent it would go to Dolores if Joe were dead. The examples of accidents Vera gives Dolores make us realize that Vera was responsible for her own husband's deadly automobile accident. Vera's fascination with the eclipse gives Dolores an idea. If she kills Joe when the islanders are distracted by the eclipse, no one will see her. Dolores carefully prepares her plan. King is confident that the obstacles she has to overcome will reinforce our sympathy for her. With most fictional murders we are concerned about the victim. In this case we want Dolores to get away with it. We appreciate that she sees no other way to deal with her problems, and as far as we can see, Joe has no redeeming qualities.

Even though we know Dolores has killed Joe, King manages to create tension as the eclipse approaches. Joe almost succeeds in climbing out of the well she tricks him into, and Dolores has to hit him with a rock to get him back down into it. We immediately worry about what will happen when he is found, fearing that the blow from the rock may incriminate Dolores. Even after the murder the suspense does not end. Dolores worries that no one will discover the body. Once it is discovered she has to face questioning by a suspicious county medical examiner, Dr. John McAuliffe, Dolores thinks of how Vera would handle this situation and is able to avoid saying anything incriminating. No one knows about the money, so no motive is obvious. But just as Vera has lost the love of her children, Dolores knows that Selena suspects her of killing Joe, and she has lost her daughter's love.

King brings us to Vera's final day. For years she has lived in terror of the dust bunnies under her bed. King suggests that they are connected to her guilt over her husband's death and her pain over the later deaths of her two children. On her last day she is so afraid that she manages to get out of her wheelchair, to which she has been confined, and falls down the stairs before Dolores can reach her. Vera is dying, and she asks Dolores to help her die faster. Dolores gets the rolling pin from the kitchen, but by the time she returns Vera is dead. The mailman, who arrives on the scene and sees her with the rolling pin, starts the talk about Dolores killing Vera. This time, although she doesn't know it, Dolores has a motive because Vera has left her almost all of her estate, 30 million dollars. Her listeners and King's readers believe Dolores's story. We learn that she is absolved of responsibility from the first article in the Scrapbook which closes the novel, describing the result of the coroner's inquest. It is followed by excerpts from two other articles. The first tells of a mystery donation of 30 million dollars to the New England Home for Little Wanderers, the charity to which Vera had already left part of her estate. This explains what Dolores has done with her inheritance. The last article tells of the upcoming Christmas celebration Dolores is preparing for Joe Junior and his family, who will be joined by Selena. This suggests that Selena may have finally forgiven her mother. The Scrapbook thus brings us back to the present. King does not want another voice to follow Dolores's. Unlike most King novels, all of the questions it has raised are answered. All of its conflicts are neatly resolved.

## Rose Madder

*Rose Madder* opens with a startling description of Rose McClendon Daniels sitting in a corner having a miscarriage as a result of an attack by her husband, Norman. The events are described from her point of view and we gradually figure out what has happened. Her husband has come home and found her reading a book he doesn't like, *Misery's Journey*. King readers recognize the title as one from the series by Paul Sheldon, the author in *Misery*. The novel is not the real cause of the attack. There is no reason, no cause; he just does it. We watch as he cleans up the evidence before the ambulance arrives, eating a sandwich as he wipes up her blood. He is a policeman and knows about evidence and the questions which may be asked. As the prologue ends we move on to even more horrifying information. King tells us that people who are awake know about dreaming, but dreamers don't know the real world. We learn that Rose has not left her husband: "Rose McClendon Daniels slept with her husband's madness for nine more years" (9).

King summarizes the abuse Rose has experienced during the fourteen years of her marriage. We are amazed at what she has survived. The casual way the three or four beatings a year which send her to bed are presented makes us aware of the hopelessness of her world. The pattern is so set that she can see no way out of it. Small details such as the year 1985 and the name Wendy Yarrow became important later in the novel. The words on Norman's Police Academy ring, "Service, Loyalty, Community," are ironically connected to wife abuse. The incident which is the last straw for Rose and finally makes her decide to leave her husband is something small, a single drop of blood on her sheet from a nosebleed.

We share Rose's fears as she takes Norman's ATM card and sets out before she can change her mind. Rose dates her new life from the moment she finally gets into a cab and goes to the bus terminal. She decides she is no longer Rose Daniels but Rosie McClendon, the girl she was before she married. We watch carefully, hoping she has not left any clues for Norman to follow. While she is innocent about life because she has spent so little time outside her house, she is familiar with police methods.

The narrative moves between the two central characters, Rose, trying to establish a new life for herself, and Norman, trying to track her down. A new phase of her life begins when Rosie goes to pawn her wedding ring and learns it is a fake. The pawnshop is a special place for her. Bill Steiner, who waits on her, later becomes her lover and her husband. Another man in the store, Robbie Lefferts, loves her voice and hires her for a new career—recording books. As she wanders around the store she is drawn to an oil painting. While she recognizes that it is not very good, the image of the woman in a toga standing on top of a hill looking at the ruins of a temple attracts her. We can see only the woman's back, but she seems to be shading her eyes. On the back of the painting are the words "rose madder," but she knows rose madder probably refers to the color of the woman's dress. Rosie likes the connection with her name and trades her ring for the painting.

Every time we encounter Norman he commits another violent act, heightening the suspense. We learn that he has strangled a prostitute because she looked like Rosie. We also learn that several years ago he beat a woman named Wendy Yarrow during questioning, and it turned out he had the wrong apartment. Norman killed her before she could pursue her court case against him. Norman follows Rosie by trying to become her, doing things the way she would. Norman's cunning and cruelty make us fear him. King increases the suspense by having Norman kill people we like. We don't know whom he will get next, and we don't like to see the deaths of people we admire. Up to this point in the novel the horror has all been realistic. Norman is a monster, but he is a human monster.

King introduces the supernatural as Rosie's picture changes slightly every time she looks at it.

She is increasingly influenced by the painting, dying her hair blond and plaiting it to resemble that of the woman in the rose madder toga. One night Rosie wakes up and sees the painting covering a wall in her apartment. Figures in the painting move. She enters the strange world of the painting and looks back at her room, which is now a painting on an easel. This is the first of two journeys Rosie takes in the imaginary world of the painting.

The two trips are like mythic journeys in fairy tales or quest novels. The first experience may consist of a series of tests or tasks the character must master. The second trip may be a final trial or may be the point when the character is rewarded for what has been learned during the first test. King uses a variety of names and symbols in the world of the painting. Rosie's entry into this world also brings to mind Alice's trip through the looking-glass. Some of Rosie's encounters echo elements of the real world, the way Dorothy's experiences in Oz recall characters from Kansas. We can also view Rosie's adventure as a kind of living dream where people in the real world turn up as characters.

Rosie recognizes the first woman she meets, her guide, as Wendy Yarrow. She tells Rosie what she must do, and gives her the information she needs to survive. After meeting Rose Madder, the woman on the hill, Rosie thinks she is in a dream. Rosie discovers that Rose Madder is an imperfect mirror image of herself; something is wrong with her skin and her voice. We later understand that Rose Madder is also an image of the rage inside Rosie. Wendy gives Rosie the tools for her journey. As with any magical trip Rosie must avoid certain traps to reach her goal. Wendy soaks one strip of Rosie's nightgown in her own blood to help Rosie fool the sense of smell of the one-eyed, blind bull, Erinyes. (In Greek mythology, the Erinyes, or Furies, originally hunted cursed criminals. "Erinyes" comes from the Greek word meaning hunting down or persecuting and is a word indicating anger [*Harper's Dictionary of Classical*

*Literature and Antiquities*, s.v. "Eumenides."]) Wendy's blood turns the cloth the color rose madder. Rosie wraps the strip around a stone and puts it in the rest of her nightgown which she has taken off.

Rosie must pass through the temple of death and cross a stream by stepping-stones without ever touching the poisoned water. Then she must walk through a grove of trees, dead except for one, and get the seeds from the fruit of the living tree without even putting her finger in her mouth. She also must not drink from the stream. Rosie must then go down some stairs and into a maze, where she will find a baby. She has to evade the bull who inhabits the maze and return with the baby. Rosie, strengthened by the courage she developed through years of living with Norman, manages to accomplish all her tasks. She is tempted to drink from the stream of forgetfulness so that she will no longer remember her past, but she realizes she would forget Bill as well. She calls the baby Caroline, the name chosen for the baby she lost.

When Rosie returns to Wendy and Rose with the baby, Wendy tells her that it is important to forget the past. Wendy shares part of her own past with Rosie by mentioning the city of Lud (the same city found in *The Waste Lands*; see Chapter 7). She tells Rosie, "It ain't the blows we're dealt that matter, but the ones we survive" (232). Wendy also tells her not to look at Rose's face. Rose takes the baby, talks with Rosie about men, and promises to repay her. Rosie returns to her bed. When she finds evidence of her adventures, the armlet and a packet with three remaining seeds, she realizes that she has not been dreaming, and hopes she's not losing her mind.

When she wakens, Rosie also senses that Norman is thinking about her. But she does not let these thoughts prevent her from going on a picnic with Bill. King uses this scene to introduce the last element Rosie needs to free herself from her past. On the picnic Bill shows her a vixen and her kits. When she looks at the fox Rosie recalls Wendy's caution about not looking at Rose's face. King uses this device to associate Rose and the vixen. Rosie knows if they touched the kits, the red fox would also repay as Rose has promised. Bill says the foxes will be OK if they do not go mad with rabies. When we think of madness we think of Rose Madder and connect her more closely with the red fox. Bill tells Rosie that a vixen can carry the sickness a long time before it emerges.

The narrative returns to Norman, who is discovered at the Daughters and Sisters shelter's fundraising event. He fights with two women who are members of the shelter, and steals a Ferdinand the bull mask. The injured women go to the hospital, and Rosie and Bill, who learn of the attack, meet them there. Rosie finally talks to the police. She identifies the man they are looking for: "He's my husband, he's a police detective, and he's crazy" (302). We hope the police will be able to track him before he kills anyone else. But we know there will have to be some kind of final meeting between him and Rosie and Rose Madder.

The bull, talking with the voice of an oracle, gives Norman information about Rosie. Norman finally catches up with Rosie in her apartment. He attacks Rosie and Bill, who manage to get to her room and slip into the painting, followed by Norman. Norman wears the bull mask and can only see out of one eye. Once he enters the world of the painting he cannot remove the mask. He has become the bull, Erinyes. Rosie lures Norman to the clearing with the fruit tree where Rose is waiting. While we know he is the real monster, she looks like a monster to him. Rose draws him to her using the words Norman always used before he beat Rosie: "I want to talk to you, and I want to talk to you right . . . up . . . CLOSE!" As King tells us, "Norman finally learned what it was like to be the bitten instead of the biter" (381). She repays Rosie by killing Norman. Rosie does look at Rose and sees many things, including the face of a fox. In this scene, King has put all of the major characters and events together.

Once Norman is dead we might expect the story to be over, but Rosie's problems are not resolved. Rose gives Rosie Norman's police ring as a souvenir and tells her to remember the tree. Rosie realizes that she needs her dreams; she doesn't want to forget. The story cannot end until Rosie deals with her memories. She throws out two of the seeds she has brought with her but keeps one. King moves us quickly through her wedding to Bill, her pregnancy, and the birth of Pamela Gertrude, to the point where her anger begins to surface. Rosie can barely control herself until the night she dreams of the tree and realizes that she has been thinking of the wrong tree. She returns to the picnic area and goes to the tree where she saw the vixen. This tree and the one in the painting are the same. In an act associated with magical stories, Rosie buries the last seed in the circle of her husband's ring. The vixen appears. When Rosie leaves the tree, the fox lies down on the spot where she buried the objects. Rosie looks at her and sees both madness and sanity. Rosie is finally at peace, but she returns once a year to watch the new tree grow. The novel ends with the image of the old vixen who listens to Rosie sing in the clearing. "Her black eyes as she stands there communicate no clear thought to Rosie, but it is impossible to mistake the essential sanity of the old and clever brain behind them" (420).

## CHARACTERS

The characters in *Dolores Claiborne* and *Rose Madder* fall into two groups: women who have been abused and male abusers. All the other characters support either one group or the other. But King does not make the divisions simply along gender lines. Little Joe supports Dolores, and the police who listen to her story do not condemn her. In addition to Bill, the police who track Norman also support Rosie. The abusers have very few companions. Joe has buddies in *Dolores Claiborne,* and Norman has his partner and other police buddies in *Rose Madder*. But King fails to develop these secondary characters. In contrast, many of those who help Dolores and Rosie have interesting personalities, even though we may know them for only a short time. While there are fewer characters in *Dolores Claiborne,* we get a sense of those who listen to her story during the course of the novel.

### The Women

The women in the two novels can be arranged on a scale from most to least in control of their lives. Those with the least control are the central characters, and they learn how to gain power over their lives during the course of the novel. In these works King concentrates on moments of crisis in the lives of his central characters. We learn about their personalities by observing how they deal with stress. It is an indication of King's growth as an author that he can comfortably present the inner worlds of these female characters. Dolores tells us her story, and Rosie's actions are presented from her point of view. Both women endure a lot from their husbands. For each there is a turning point where they make a stand. When Joe hits her with a piece of wood, Dolores realizes that she may not survive more beating. Rosie, seeing the drop of blood on her sheet, suddenly understands that if the beating goes on Norman will kill her.

Rosie is the character who suffers the most and changes the most. She moves from being the person with the least hope to the one with the greatest possibility for happiness. While we get some sense of Rosie's past, we see only one point in her earlier life. King examines a period of crisis in her life in the greatest detail and then presents selected later moments. He shows Dolores over a longer span of time, but concentrates on events which mark the changes in her life. Once she survives her crisis, he examines the results very briefly. Both these women face alone those moments where their lives will change. They have assistance from others in implementing these decisions, but ultimately they have to make critical choices on their own.

In addition to the moments when they must deal with their abuser, both women must also react to the people they like. While Dolores may not admit it, she has a significant relationship with Vera. She balances the action she takes in killing Joe with her willingness to end Vera's life for her. King shows that the motivation for an act is more important than the act itself. Rosie's transformation is not complete until she deals with her rage. She has to acknowledge how she feels. At first she merely tries to direct her rage away from those she cares for. But she realizes that it cannot be contained and that she could actually be a threat to her new husband. King shows that anger is a negative emotion even in a good character. Rosie must let go of her past to live in the present. Dolores deals with her past through confession. For both women, these actions allow them to regain or retain the good in their lives. Rosie is able to control her anger, and Dolores is reconciled with her daughter.

The other women in the novels support the central characters. Some, like Vera, represent an extreme version of Dolores. She shows Dolores what she needs to do to change her situation. But Vera's actions are less justified. She kills her husband because he is cheating on her. She never recovers from this action because she also loses her children, who die in an automobile accident. Vera never deals with her past and ends her life both spiritually and physically paralyzed. She is tortured by her memories and loses most of her mental abilities. Only at the end does she once again briefly act and think clearly. While Dolores remains connected to Vera through much of both of their lives, Rosie loses two important women almost immediately after forming a relationship with them. Rosie's relationship with the women in the novel is like her experience with her unborn daughter, Caroline. She is four months pregnant when Norman causes the miscarriage. He also kills Pam, her first friend in her new life. Anna Stevenson is not a close friend, but King suggests the importance of their relationship through their shared taste in fiction. Rosie notices that Anna also reads books in the *Misery* series. When she sees the cover on Anna's desk Rosie recalls the book as the source of Norman's rage the day of the miscarriage. Anna becomes another one of

Norman's victims. While all of these women are important, the secondary characters are most important because of what they represent for Rosie and Dolores.

### The Men

The two husbands differ only in the degree of violence they demonstrate. Joe is less cunning and less violent than Norman. But he attempts to molest his daughter, an act King seems to find almost as evil as murder. King connects Joe's murder with the child molestation in *Gerald's Game*, suggesting that Joe represents the kind of man, unfortunately too common, whose actions cause so much pain for their wives and children. He also shares certain traits with Norman. Both men are bigots who constantly make racist, homophobic, and anti-Semitic statements. They are bullies who abuse women because they can. They see violence as the only way to react to the frustrations in their lives.

While characters like Joe are found in the background of many King novels, Norman's violence is so extreme that he is actually a kind of monstrous killing machine. In *The Shining*, Jack demonstrates some of the same anger, but his is also stimulated by contact with the ghosts in the hotel. Like many of King's abusers and victims, Norman has been beaten by his father. King shows how a chain of abuse is developed. Joe is violent, but he is not very smart. Norman's savagery goes far beyond that of any other King character. Norman's extreme violence is especially frightening because he is a member of the police force. An expert at tracking criminals, he also uses his skill to track his victims. We are also horrified because police are supposed to help maintain the morality of society, and Norman has no morals. We do not mourn the death of either man. We can forget Joe. We know there are Joes everywhere. We are relieved that Norman is gone. But we are not very reassured. If we have met one Norman, do others also exist?

## THEME

In *Rose Madder* and *Dolores Claiborne* King introduces new themes and develops traditional ones. He presents the new themes of the role of anger and the importance of dreams in the characters' lives. He continues to explore the roles of destiny and fate and the idea of the personal quest.

He examines the relationship between evil and the supernatural. King also continues to develop feminist concerns (see the Alternate Reading section, below). One of King's strengths is his refusal to repeat the same fictional formulas in work after work. His most recent novels fully demonstrate the extent to which his work is constantly evolving.

As King matures, his characters also grow up. His early works examine the parent/child relationship and stress the importance of retaining a child's imagination as an adult. The mature King no longer fears the loss of imaginative powers with maturity. Children are not important in his recent books. Dolores's concern over her children may push her toward action, but the children do not play major roles. In this novel parents must face the possibility that their actions may sever a relationship with their children. Parents may regret these actions, but King does not condemn them. Both Dolores and Vera suffer from their children's suspicions. Both women must work out the guilt these doubts cause. But King is interested in the women and their reactions rather than the children. We never see the action from a child's point of view.

Children are not particularly significant in *Rose Madder* either. Rosie's miscarriage is important in her life, but this loss is not what gives her the courage to leave her husband. In her first journey into the painting she retrieves a child who is symbolic of Rose Madder's loss. She gives this child the name she had chosen for the baby she lost. But children are not central to her interaction with the painting. She faces the supernatural as an adult, and the horrors she faces are those that only an adult can confront. Her fears and her anger are the result of her relationship with her husband. But she is attracted to the painting on her own. She buys it because it speaks to her adult concerns, not because it has any connection with her childhood.

We learn little about the childhood of the central characters in either novel. King tells only enough about Dolores's youth to explain her marriage. He acknowledges that adult abusers were often the recipients of abuse in childhood, but the women's lives really begin when they awaken to the possibilities of adult action. They finally understand what it means to be an adult and make decisions and take action once they see possibilities which have been hidden by the stupor of their lives.

King tells us that Rosie lived through her life with Norman in a daze, hoping to wake up in another life. He also describes Rosie's life with Norman as a kind of dream with no reference points in the real world. She must awaken from her stupor to save herself. Rosie has to get to the point where she can move into the real world to escape from Norman.

But she must also return to a kind of dream when she enters the painting and finally rids herself of him. Dolores often moves through her life in a kind of daze. She awakens only when Joe pushes her too far. Dolores kills Joe during an eclipse—that rare moment when day is night. If dreams usually occur at night when we sleep, Dolores makes real her dream of a life without Joe when day and night reverse themselves. Both women awaken to the real world when they realize that unless they do something, their husbands will kill them. Dolores kills Joe, and the book explores the effects of that action. Rosie does not kill Norman, but in a sense her anger leads him to his death. She finally deals with her anger at the very end of the book.

Dolores's anger is not just focused on Joe. There is a great deal of anger in her love/hate relationship with Vera, who also abuses Dolores. Because Dolores expresses her anger toward Vera, she is accused of murder. King suggests that people who work through their anger end up respecting each other even if they don't become friends. Vera and Dolores finally do respect each other. Rosie never has the opportunity to acknowledge her anger toward Norman because her fear of him freezes all other emotions. The painting becomes her first means of expressing her anger. Rosie thinks of the woman in the painting as Rose Madder, and we understand that she is the "madder" version of Rosie in both sense of the word. Rosie must do what Rose cannot, and Rose assures Rosie that she will repay her for her efforts. Ultimately Rose will do what Rosie cannot.

By the end of *Rose Madder* Rosie finally buries her anger toward Norman because she is in danger of being consumed by it. Rosie must move from the dream world of the painting to the real world of the vixen, who is another image of madness in the novel. The world of the painting merges into the real world when Rosie buries Norman's ring next to the same tree as the one in the painting. The vixen stays by the tree, and when Rosie visits her, the fox has not gone insane. Rosie and the vixen retain their sanity in the face of the stresses of the real world. Rosie needed Rose Madder to confront Norman and destroy him, but she needs the real world to heal her own anger.

While King's novels are generally plot-driven, recently he has begun to explore the role of destiny in characters' lives. In a carefully plotted novel events must be planned so that the reader makes the correct connections and the work moves in the intended direction. King balances his role as the creator of the action with that of his characters, whose decisions must motivate the action. In the early novels King works out this relationship separately for each work. In some of his recent novels he refers to a cosmic organization first presented in *The Dark Tower* series. Rose Madder explains the role of fate when she tells Rosie that she will be divorced from Norman. Rose says that some men may be controlled, but others are like beasts. When we meet one of these rogues we should not curse our fate. "Should we rage against *ka*? No, for *ka* is the wheel that moves the world, and the man or woman who rages against it will be crushed under its rim" (233). The image of the wheel which moves the world suggests inevitability, a kind of predestination governing our lives. Both the image of the wheel and the idea of *ka* are introduced in *The Dark Tower* series. But in all King's novels characters are free to take actions which can improve their situations.

In *Dolores Claiborne* and *Rose Madder* the characters are placed in certain roles through the action of fate or destiny. But each woman must decide to act if she is going to change her direction. It may do no good to rage against *ka*, but we can make choices which will alter our lives. Of course we can further question the concept of free will because, as author, King determines the way the characters will act and the choices they will make. But he makes us believe that the characters have real choices and that the plot could move in any direction. Rosie and Dolores must confront the evil in their lives, but they can make choices about how they will deal with it.

In *Dolores Claiborne* and *Rose Madder* King continues the examination of the nature of evil which forms the core of much of his work. In both novels evil has a human rather than a supernatural source. King continues to support those who respond to evil by destroying it. A certain amount of violence seems to be necessary to overcome such malignancy when it appears. But anyone who uses violence is contaminated by it. Rosie and Dolores have to work to eliminate the remnants of anger left by their actions. While they are individuals and respond to individual actions, the evil they fight is connected to the wider world and the universe of King's fiction. King connects Dolores's experiences with those of Jessie in *Gerald's Game*. They have visions of one another at key moments when they are either suffering or dealing directly with their problems. The concept of *ka*, or destiny, in *Rose Madder* connects the book to *The Dark Tower* series and *Insomnia*. Wendy tells Rosie about her past in Lud, a city in *The Waste Lands*. Wendy has seen much in the company of Rose Madder. She looks back from her days as a slave into the future world of *The Dark Tower.* Just before Vera helps Dolores arrive at the idea of killing Joe, Dolores sees her employer as one of the three fates, Atropos. This name is associated with random death in *Insomnia.*

Often the supernatural is the source of evil in a King novel. The only suggestions of a world beyond the real in *Dolores Claiborne* are the visions of Dolores and Jessie of *Gerald's Game* and their connections to the shared eclipse. While the eclipse is a natural phenomenon, it has mystical meanings as well. By uniting two novels with a single event King gives the eclipse magical power. An eclipse appears to upset the natural order of the universe by interrupting the orderly progression of day and night. In both novels the eclipse provokes an unnatural action. Jessie's father molests her while she sits on his lap observing the eclipse. Dolores uses the eclipse to find privacy on a crowded island and kill her husband. In both novels, once the eclipse is over the characters attempt to return to their normal lives. But the unnatural effects of the eclipse follow them until they can finally resolve the problems raised by their encounter with evil during the eclipse.

*Rose Madder* seems to be a realistic novel until Rosie buys the painting. In this novel and *Dolores Claiborne* King shows the horror which comes from our world. He still has no explanation beyond *ka,* the wheel of destiny, to explain why some people suffer. When the source of human suffering takes the form of someone like Norman, it is just as irrational as supernatural evil. The references to *Misery,* which contains another example of how human madness leads to evil, further demonstrate the horrors of the real world. Recently King seems to be more concerned about the evil human beings do to each other than what the monsters of his imagination can do to them.

In *Rose Madder* the supernatural is the place where evil is destroyed. Rose Madder destroys Norman. She and Wendy give Rosie the information she needs to finally bring her life under control and deal with her memories and her anger. When Rosie buries her husband's ring and plants the seed, this ritual brings healing. Rose Madder may represent Rosie's rage, but she gives Rosie the means to conquer that rage. The supernatural does not create the evil in our lives. In *Rose Madder* and *Dolores Claiborne* King continues to examine the randomness of some of the bad things that happen. He also explores the ways in which humans can be more evil than the worst monster.

## ALTERNATE READING: FEMINISM

When we look at literature from a feminist perspective we examine how women are treated in the fiction, how their images are presented, and the kinds of issues the author raises. Positive images of women show them in active roles; such women take control of their lives. They have the power to make important decisions. Novels that present positive images of women consider all aspects of their lives important and do not depict women as inferiors. Plots can also affect the image of women. Some stories portray women as victims with no sense of choice about what happens to them. Women may also be seen as evil—as causing all the problems in the novel.

In three recent novels with women as the central character—*Gerald's Game, Dolores Claiborne,* and *Rose Madder*—King demonstrates how far he has come in his ability to create convincing female characters. He has used women's names as the titles of four of his novels: *Carrie, Christine, Dolores Claiborne,* and *Rose Madder*. King does not consider *Carrie,* his first novel, an effective presentation of a woman's point of view. In *Christine,* the woman's name refers to an evil car. *Dolores Claiborne* and *Rose Madder* use the full names of women, one real and one imaginary. By extension *Rose Madder* also refers to the central character, Rosie McClendon, who is her mirror image. The only novel to use a man's name, *Gerald's Game,* is actually about a woman. In these three novels King has developed characters who are the center of the novel and control the action. *Gerald's Game* provides a transition to the more complex examinations of the full range of women's lives found in *Rose Madder* and *Dolores Claiborne*. In both novels King depicts a number of interesting women, who operate both alone and together as they work through the problems in their lives.

*Dolores Claiborne* and *Rose Madder* depict women who can live on their own, independent of men. Dolores and Rosie learn to develop single lives. Vera, too, lives for many years managing the fortune her husband left her. She does have a lover, but he plays such a small role that we barely know his name. We might also be concerned that Rosie finds a new man so quickly. But from the first time we see her she is overwhelmed by the loss of her child. We also observe her with Bill. She has grown to the point where they seem to have a marriage in which everything is shared. Rosie also keeps her job after she is married. King shows us how their children will follow their example when he presents Selena, Dolores's daughter, as a successful young woman.

The women in *Rose Madder* and *Dolores Claiborne* also have a sense of community. Both Dolores and Rosie call on their images of other women to help them get through moments of crisis. In the Daughters and Sisters women's shelter King shows women working together to overcome the trauma of abuse. He shows characters who are physically as well as mentally powerful. The women in both novels demonstrate a great range of behavior. Vera may not be a pleasant person, but we understand her view of the world and appreciate her toughness. As she says to Dolores just before the eclipse, "Sometimes being a bitch is all a woman has to hold onto" (169). Dolores describes the ways in which Vera is a bitch, but she has sympathy for Vera because she understands the reasons behind Vera's actions. Rosie does not really like Anna, but she respects Anna's dedication to the organization she has created, Daughters and Sisters.

King demonstrates a great deal of concern about all types of abuse. He has always condemned fathers who abuse their daughters and husbands who abuse their wives. But now he shows women who can take action against abuse. While he creates women who fight back, he also explores the effects of unexpressed anger. He shows that rage must come out. Women have to deal with the memories of their abusive relationships. He also examines how abusive partnerships poison the whole family. His men are the children of abusers, and his women have trouble keeping their children's love when they fight back. But King also shows that the battle is worth it. By the end of *Dolores Claiborne* and *Rose Madder* both women have achieved peace with themselves and with their children. King's positive endings are another example of his view of women's issues. The struggle may be difficult in King's recent fiction, but women who work through their crises have a chance at happiness.

# Bibliography

## WORKS BY STEPHEN KING

*Note*: Page numbers referred to in the text are to the paperback editions of Stephen King's novels, with the exception of the following: *Needful Things, Insomnia, Dolores Claiborne*, and *Rose Madder*. These page references are to the hardcover editions of the books.

### Novels

*Carrie*. Garden City, NY: Doubleday, 1974; New York: New American Library, 1975.

*Christine*. New York: Viking, 1983; New York: Signet, 1983.

*Cujo*. New York: Viking, 1981; New York: Signet, 1982.

*Cycle of the Wolf*. Westland, MI: Land of Enchantment, 1983; New York: New American Library, 1985.

*The Dark Half*. New York: Viking, 1989; New York: New American Library, 1990.

*The Dark Tower: The Gunslinger*. West Kingston, RI: Donald M. Grant, 1984; New York: New American Library, 1988.

*The Dark Tower II: The Drawing of the Three*. New York: New American Library, 1987.

*The Dark Tower III: The Waste Lands*. New York: New American Library, 1991.

*The Dead Zone*. New York: Viking Press, 1979; New York: New American Library, 1980.

*Dolores Claiborne*. New York: Viking, 1993; New York: New American Library, 1994.
*The Eyes of the Dragon*. New York: Viking, 1987; New York: New American Library, 1987.
*Firestarter*. New York: Viking, 1980; New York: New American Library, 1981.
*Gerald's Game*. New York: Viking, 1992; New York: New American Library, 1993.
*Insomnia*. New York: Viking, 1994; New York: New American Library, 1995.
*It*. New York: Viking, 1986; New York: New American Library, 1987.
*Misery*. New York: Viking, 1987; New York: New American Library, 1987.
*Needful Things*. New York: Viking, 1991; New York: New American Library, 1992.
*Pet Sematary*. Garden City, NY: Doubleday, 1983; New York: New American Library, 1984.
*Rose Madder*. New York: Viking, 1995.
*'Salem's Lot*. Garden City, NY: Doubleday, 1975; New York: New American Library, 1976.
*The Shining*. Garden City, NY: Doubleday, 1977; New York: New American Library, 1978.
*The Stand*. Garden City, NY: Doubleday, 1978; New York: New American Library, 1979; 2nd ed., rev. and unexpurg., New York: Doubleday, 1990.
[With Peter Straub.] *The Talisman*. New York: Viking Press and G. P. Putnam's Sons, 1984; New York: Berkley, 1985.
*The Tommyknockers*. New York: G. P. Putnam's Sons, 1987; New York: New American Library, 1988.

## Stephen King Writing as Richard Bachman

*The Long Walk*. New York: New American Library, 1979.
*Rage*. New York: New American Library, 1977.
*Roadwork*. New York: New American Library, 1981.
*The Running Man*. New York: New American Library, 1982.
*Thinner*. New York: New American Library, 1984.

## Collections

*The Bachman Books: Four Early Novels*. New York: New American Library, 1985.
*Creepshow*. New York: New American Library, 1982.
*Different Seasons*. New York: Viking, 1982; New York: New American Library, 1983.
*Four Past Midnight*. New York: Viking, 1990; New York: New American Library, 1991.

*Night Shift*. Garden City, NY: Doubleday, 1978; New York: New American Library, 1983.
*Nightmares and Dreamscapes*. New York: Viking, 1993.
*Skeleton Crew*. New York: Putnam, 1985; New York: New American Library, 1986.

### Nonfiction

*Danse Macabre*. New York: Everest House, 1981; New York: Berkley, 1982.
"On Becoming a Brand Name," Foreword to *Fear Itself: The Early Works of Stephen King*. Ed. Tim Underwood and Chuck Miller. San Francisco: Underwood-Miller, 1993: 15–42.
"Son of the Best Seller Stalks the Moors." *New York Times Book Review*, 6 June 1993, sec. 7:59.

### Screenplays

*Cat's Eye*
*Creepshow*
*Golden Years*
*Maximum Overdrive*
*Pet Sematary*
*Silver Bullet*
*Sleepwalkers*
*The Stand*

## WORKS ABOUT STEPHEN KING

### General

Beahm, George, ed. *The Stephen King Companion*. Kansas City, MO: Andrews and McMeel, 1989.
Blue, Tyson. *The Unseen King*. Mercer Island, WA: Starmont House, 1989.
Browne, Ray, and Gary Hoppenstand, eds. *The Gothic World of Stephen King: Landscape of Nightmares*. Bowling Green, OH: Bowling Green State University Popular Press, 1987.
Burns, Gail E. "Women, Danger, and Death: The Perversion of the Female Principle in Stephen King's Fiction." In *Sexual Politics and Popular Culture*. Ed. Diane Raymond. Bowling Green, OH: Bowling Green State University Popular Press, 1990: 158–72.

Collings, Michael R. *The Films of Stephen King*. Mercer Island, WA: Starmont House, 1986.

———. *Infinite Explorations: Art and Artifice in Stephen King's* It, Misery, *and* The Tommyknockers. Mercer Island, WA: Starmont House, 1986.

———. *The Many Facets of Stephen King*. Mercer Island, WA: Starmont House, 1985.

———. *Stephen King as Richard Bachman*. Mercer Island, WA: Starmont House, 1985.

———. *The Stephen King Concordance*. Mercer Island, WA: Starmont House, 1985.

———. *The Stephen King Phenomenon*. Mercer Island, WA: Starmont House, 1986.

Collings, Michael R., and David A. Engebretson. *The Shorter Works of Stephen King*. Mercer Island, WA: Starmont House, 1985.

Connor, Jeff. *Stephen King Goes to Hollywood*. New York: New American Library, 1987.

Davis, Jonathan P. *Stephen King's America*. Bowling Green, OH: Bowling Green University Popular Press, 1994.

Docherty, Brian, ed. *American Horror Fiction: From Brockden Brown to Stephen King*. New York: St. Martin's, 1990.

Egan, James. "Apocalypticism in the Fiction of Stephen King." *Extrapolation* 25 (1984): 214–27.

———. "Sacral Parody in the Fiction of Stephen King." *Journal of Popular Culture* 23 (Winter 1989): 125–41.

———. " 'A Single Powerful Spectacle': Stephen King's Gothic Melodrama." *Extrapolation* 27 (1986): 62–75.

Gallagher, Bernard J. "Breaking Up Isn't Hard to Do: Stephen King, Christopher Lasch, and Psychic Fragmentation." *Journal of American Culture* 10 (Winter 1987): 59–67.

Herron, Don, ed. *Reign of Fear: Fiction and Film of Stephen King*. Los Angeles: Underwood-Miller, 1988.

Hohne, Karen A. "The Power of the Spoken Word in the Works of Stephen King." *Journal of Popular Culture* 28, no. 2 (1994): 93–103.

Horsting, Jessie. *Stephen King at the Movies*. New York: Starlog Press and New American Library, 1986.

Lloyd, Ann. *The Films of Stephen King*. New York: St. Martin's, 1994.

Magistrale, Tony, ed. *The Dark Descent: Essays Defining Stephen King's Horrorscape*. Westport, CT: Greenwood Press, 1992.

———. "Inherited Haunts: Stephen King's Terrible Children." *Extrapolation* 26 (1985): 43–49.

———. *Landscape of Fear: Stephen King's American Gothic*. Bowling Green, OH: Bowling Green State University Popular Press, 1988.

———. *The Moral Voyages of Stephen King*. Mercer Island, WA: Starmont House, 1989.

———. *Stephen King, the Second Decade:* Danse Macabre *to* The Dark Half. New York: Twayne, 1992.

Price, Robert M. "Fundamentalists in the Fiction of Stephen King." *Studies-in-Weird-Fiction* (Spring 1989): 12–14.

Reino, Joseph. *Stephen King, the First Decade: From* Carrie *to* Pet Sematary. Boston: Twayne, 1988.

Schweitzer, Darrell, ed. *Discovering Stephen King*. Mercer Island, WA: Starmont House, 1985.

Spignesi, Stephen J. *The Complete Stephen King Encyclopedia*. Ann Arbor, MI: Popular Culture, Ink, 1993.

Underwood, Tim, and Chuck Miller, eds. *Fear Itself: The Early Works of Stephen King*. San Francisco: Underwood-Miller, 1993.

———. *Kingdom of Fear: The World of Stephen King*. New York: New American Library, 1986.

Winter, Douglas E. *The Reader's Guide to Stephen King*. Mercer Island, WA: Starmont House, 1982.

———. *Stephen King: The Art of Darkness*. New York: New American Library, 1986.

## Biography

"Author as Star." *The Economist* 310 (18 March 1989): 97.

Beahm, George. *The Stephen King Story*. Kansas City, MO: Andrews and McMeel, 1992.

Caldwell, Gail. "Stephen King: Bogeyman as Family Man." *Boston Globe*, 15 April 1990: 1A+.

Davis, William A. "The Horror King of Bangor." *Boston Globe*, 31 October 1990: 25.

Denison. D. C. "Stephen King." *Boston Globe*, 2 August 1987: 2.

Geyelin, Milo, and Wade Lambert. "Stephen King." *Wall Street Journal*, 5 October 1992: 3B.

Golden, Daniel, "Field of Screams." *Boston Globe*, 30 August 1992: 14 BGM+.

"King Haunted by College Columns." *Boston Globe*, 5 December 1990: 73.

Underwood, Tim, and Chuck Miller, eds. *Bare Bones: Conversations on Terror with Stephen King*. New York: Warner Books, 1989.

———. *Feast of Fear: Conversation with Stephen King*. New York: Warner Books, 1993.

## *'Salem's Lot*

Reino, Joseph. "The Dracula Myth: Shadow and Substance." In *Stephen King, the First Decade: From* Carrie *to* Pet Sematary. Boston: Twayne, 1988: 18–33.

Ryan, Alan. "The Marsten House in 'Salem's Lot." In *Fear Itself: The Early Works of Stephen King*. Ed. Tim Underwood and Chuck Miller. San Francisco: Underwood-Miller, 1993: 169–80.

Stoker, Bram. *Dracula*. Ed., intro., notes by Leonard Wolf. New York: Ballantine Books, 1975.

### *The Shining*

Curran, Ronald T. "Complex, Archetype, and Primal Fear: King's Use of Fairy Tales in *The Shining*." In *The Dark Descent: Essays Defining Stephen King's Horrorscape*. Ed. Tony Magistrale. Westport, CT: Greenwood Press, 1992: 33–46.

Magistrale, Tony, ed. The Shining *Reader*. Mercer Island, WA: Starmont House, 1991.

Yarbro, Chelsea Quinn. "Cinderella's Revenge: Twists on Fairy Tale and Mythic Themes in the Work of Stephen King." In *Fear Itself: The Early Works of Stephen King*. Ed. Tim Underwood and Chuck Miller. San Francisco: Underwood-Miller, 1993: 45–56.

### *The Stand*

Beeler, Michael. "The Book vs. the Miniseries." *Cinefantastique* 25, no. 2 (1994): 10–11.

———. "The Horror Meister." *Cinefantastique* 25, no. 2 12–13.

———. "Working with Stephen King." *Cinefantastique* 25, no. 2 16–17.

Casebeer, Edwin F. "The Three Genres of *The Stand*." In *The Dark Descent: Essays Defining Stephen King's Horrorscape*. Ed. Tony Magistrale. Westport, CT: Greenwood Press, 1992: 47–60.

Martin, Sue. " 'Stand' Corrected." *Los Angeles Times*, 15 July 1990: 12.

Whitehead, Colson. "*The Stand*." *The Voice*, 10 May 1994: 49.

Wood, Gary L. "Stephen King, the Horror Franchise." *Cinefantastique* 25, no. 2 22–23.

### *The Dark Half*

Canby, Vincent. "Pseudonym Comes to Life in a Stephen King Tale." *New York Times*, 23 April 1993: 10C.

Casebeer, Edwin F. "The Ecological System of Stephen King's *The Dark Half*." *Journal of the Fantastic in the Arts* 6.2-3 (1994): 126–42.

Travers, Peter. "Stephen King Divided." *Rolling Stone,* 13 May 1993: 113–14.

Will, George F. "The Lure of the Lurid." *Washington Post,* 10 December 1989: 7C+.

### *The Dark Tower III: The Waste Lands*

Nicholls, Richard E. "Avaunt Thee, Recreant Cyborg." *New York Times Book Review,* 29 September 1991: sec. 7:14.

*"The Waste Lands: The Dark Tower Book III." Atlanta Journal and Constitution,* 5 January 1992: 12K.

### *Needful Things*

Terry, Clifford. "Frightful 'Things' from Stephen King." *Chicago Tribune,* 27 August 1993: 7A+.

### *Insomnia*

*Encyclopedia of Occultism and Parapsychology.* Ed. Leslie A. Shepard. 2nd ed. 3 vols. Detroit: Gale Research Company, 1985, s.v. "aura," "palmistry."

*Harper's Dictionary of Classical Literature and Antiquities.* Ed. Harry Thurston Peck. New York: Cooper Square Publishers, 1963, s.v. "Moerae."

*"Insomnia." Publishers Weekly,* 1 August 1994: 69.

Rodriguez, Rene. " 'Insomnia' Proves Master of Macabre Struggling." *Terre Haute Tribune Star,* 9 October 1994: 3B.

### *Dolores Claiborne* and *Rose Madder*

Gorner, Peter. "Stephen King's Horror Comes Down to Earth." *Chicago Tribune,* 18 November 1992: sec. 5:3.

*Harper's Dictionary of Classical Literature and Antiquities.* Ed. Harry Thurston Peck. New York: Cooper Square Publishers, 1963, s.v. "Eumenides."

Kent, Bill. *"Dolores Claiborne." New York Times Book Review,* 27 December 1992: sec. 7:15.

Nicholls, Richard E. *"Rose Madder." New York Times Book Review,* 2 July 1995: 11.

Rafferty, Terrence. "Under a Cloud." *New Yorker,* 3 April 1995: 93–95.

Reed, Kit. "Will You Please Be Quiet Please?" *Washington Post,* 13 December 1992: 5WBK.

## OTHER BOOKS ON HORROR

Clover, Carol J. *Men, Women, and Chainsaws: Gender in the Modern Horror Film.* Princeton, NJ: Princeton University Press, 1992.

Heller, Terry. *The Delights of Terror: An Aesthetics of the Tale of Terror.* Urbana: University of Illinois Press, 1987.

Jackson, Rosemary. *Fantasy: The Literature of Subversion.* London: Methuen, 1981.

Todorov, Tzvetan. *The Fantastic: A Structural Approach to a Literary Genre.* Trans. Richard Howard. Ithaca, NY: Cornell University Press, 1973.

Waller, Gregory A. *American Horrors: Essays on the Modern American Horror Film.* Urbana: University of Illinois Press, 1987.

# Index

## About the Author

SHARON A. RUSSELL is Professor of Communication and Women's Studies at Indiana State University, where she also teaches film and popular culture courses. She is a former head of the Detective and Mystery Fiction section of the Popular Culture Association and a member of the International Association for the Fantastic in the Arts. She is editor of *The Dog Didn't Do It: Animals in Mystery* (forthcoming), and *A Guide to African Cinema* (forthcoming from Greenwood Press).